DION

THE WANDERER

TALKS

TRUTH

(stories, humor & music)

Dion DiMucci
WITH MIKE AQUILINA

SERVANT
BOOKS

PUBLISHED BY ST. ANTHONY MESSENGER PRESS
CINCINNATI, OHIO

Cover and book design by Mark Sullivan
Cover image ©Bill Bush

LIBRARY OF CONGRESS CATALOGING-IN-PUBLICATION DATE
Dion, 1939-
Dion : the wanderer talks truth / Dion DiMucci with Mike Aquilina.
    p. cm.
Includes bibliographical references (p.   ).
ISBN 978-0-86716-999-7 (alk. paper)
1. Dion, 1939- 2. Rock musicians—United States—Biography. 3. Christian biography. I. Aquilina, Mike. II. Title.
ML420.D56A3 2011
782.42166092—dc22
[B]
                            2011003614

ISBN 978-0-86716-999-7

Published by Servant Books, an imprint of St. Anthony Messenger Press.
28 W. Liberty St.
Cincinnati, OH 45202
www.AmericanCatholic.org
www.ServantBooks.org

Printed in the United States of America.

Printed on acid-free paper.

11 12 13 14 15   5 4 3 2 1

Dedicated
to Susan,
Tane, Lark, August,
Noah, Brittyn, and Vail

CONTENTS

FOREWORD

Lou Reed

It was 1958, and the cold winds of Long Island blew in from the ocean, their high-pitched howl mixing with the dusty, musky, mellifluous liquid sounds of rock and roll—the sounds of another life, the sounds of freedom.

As Alan Freed pounded a telephone book and the honking sax of Big Al Sears seared the airwaves with his theme song "Hand Clappin'," I sat staring at an indecipherable book on plane geometry, whose planes and angles would forever escape me. I wanted to escape it and the world of SAT tests and the college boards—and leap immediately and eternally into the world of Shirley and Lee, the Diablos, the Paragons, the Jesters, Lilian Leach and the Mellows ("Smoke from Your Cigarette"), Alicia and the Rockaways ("Why Can't I Be Loved?"—a question that certainly occupied my teenage time). The lyrics sat in my head like Shakespearean sonnets, with all the power of tragedy: "Gloria," "Why Don't You Write Me?" by the Jacks.

And then there was Dion—that great opening to "I Wonder Why" engraved in my skull forever. Dion, whose voice was unlike any other I had heard before. Dion could do all the turns, stretch those syllables so effortlessly, soar so high he could reach the sky and dance there among the stars forever.

What a voice—that had absorbed and transmogrified all these influences into his own soul, as the wine turns into blood, a voice that stood on its own remarkably and unmistakably from New York—Bronx Soul. It was the kind of voice you never forget. Over the years that voice has stayed with me, as it has, I'm sure, stayed with you. And whenever I hear it, I'm flooded with memories of what once was and what could be.

It's been my pleasure to get to know Dion over the years and even, my idea of heaven, sing occasional backup for him. He doesn't know how long I'd rehearsed those bass-line vocals. I was ready to back up Dion. He had the chops, and he practically invented the attitude. "Ruby Baby," "Donna the Prima Donna," "The Wanderer," "I'll tear open my shirt and show her 'Rosie' on my chest," a line so good that twenty-odd years later I couldn't resist doing a variant on it for one of my own albums.

After all, who could be hipper than Dion?

—from Dion's induction to the Rock and Roll
Hall of Fame, 1989

INTRODUCTION

WELL, I'VE NEVER BEEN DIAGNOSED, so I don't know if I have it. And it's been good to me anyway, so I can't really call it a disorder. But there's a certain kind of "attention deficit" that goes with the business of rock and roll. From the record-company moguls to the producers to the deejays, everybody wants you to keep your song down to three minutes and five seconds. They used to tell us it was the ideal timing for radio play.

So for most of my long life, I've been making myself tell a story as quickly as possible—in the time it takes to sing three verses with a chorus and maybe let the sax player have a few bars to show off. Brainy Russians like Tolstoy and Dostoyevsky can write fat novels so you'll get to know their favorite characters. A rock and roll singer from the Bronx has no such luxury. If I get through my allotted minutes and you don't feel like you know Donna the Prima Donna, Runaround Sue, or that guy I used to call "The Wanderer," then I'm out of luck.

I produced this book pretty much the same way I recorded my hit songs. The chapters reflect my rock and roll attention deficit. They're short and to the point. I figure I have a few minutes, at most, to sketch a character or tell a tale. I'd better make it good, or you're going to do the print-media equivalent of turning the radio dial. And since this is a book and not a record, I can't even hope for the sax player to bail me out.

The chapters are about a lot of things. They're about being a singer, songwriter, and performer. They're about growing up a sports fan in New York City in a certain time. They're about being a husband, a dad, and a grandfather. They're about being Italian-American and loving my heritage. They're about having addictions and dealing with them. They're about having very few virtues and a lot of attitude—and not dealing so well with the latter!

They're about a lot of things, but they're really about one thing. They're about Jesus Christ. In this respect at least, I'm like St. Paul: "For to me to live is Christ" (Philippians 1:21), so Jesus kind of figures in everything, from the music to the Yankees to the pasta.

I didn't always see life that way. I was a millionaire before I was twenty years old, self-made, up from poverty, and I was pretty impressed with myself. Millions of people were buying my records and listening to me on the radio. I was drinking the expensive stuff. I was dating movie starlets. I thought I had taken on the world and beaten it. I was so bright, I could live by my own light.

It's a typical rock-star attitude. The truth, however, is that I was living in darkness, falling deeper into the black pit of myself and my hungers. By my own light I couldn't see anything. I couldn't see clearly into the eyes of the people I loved, even when they were standing less than a foot away from me. I expected them to treat me the way my fans did, and I was furious when they didn't.

I'm one of the lucky rockers who lived long enough to learn that I was wrong, and that's a grace in itself. If you don't believe me, just listen to the song "Rock and Roll Heaven" by the

Righteous Brothers. They sang it in 1974 as a tribute to the rockers they'd known who had died very young: Janis Joplin, Jimi Hendrix, Jim Morrison, Otis Redding, Jim Croce, and Bobby Darin.... That was almost forty years ago, and the casualty count was already pretty high. It's gone a lot higher since then, with lots of kids dying because they believed what the record company's PR department had said about them.

I could very easily have become just another line in that Righteous Brothers song—dead from an overdose or down in a plane crash or under a car turned upside down. I gave myself enough opportunities. If I'm alive today, and if I'm writing a book about my life, its lessons and relationships, it's because I had a brush with rock mortality early on, and it made my heart, my mind, and my gut burn with a need to understand why I had survived.

So this book is a record of survival, and it's a thanksgiving for the gift. In Israel, in the days when the temple was standing, the people were supposed to go to Jerusalem whenever something good happened to them—whenever God gave them an extraordinary blessing or rescued them from dire peril. At the temple they would make a thank-offering. They would eat a meal of bread and wine with their friends, and they would "sing a new song" to the Lord.

The Church got the bread and wine thing down for me. This book is my "new song." You're my friends.

Back in 1988 I wrote a memoir with Davin Seay. It's titled *The Wanderer: Dion's Story*. The book's out there. It's on the record. So I don't intend to rehash all the details of all my professional struggles or my migrations from one record company to another. I don't need to go over every inch of the same ground I covered in that memoir. At this point in life, I'd rather be more like the cat that covers his old business than the dog that rolls in his.

I hope this book will offer a mature and considered reflection on some of the important events and people in my life. I've had some years to think about them and maybe learn a little, and I should have something to show for it. I'll also cover, for the first time, my love for the Catholic Church and my return to communion with her.

One of my great heroes is St. Augustine. He was a rock star in his own youth, back in the fourth century—a celebrity poet, very bright, who loved the ladies. He managed to get his life turned around, and he wrote about that turnaround in his great autobiography, *The Confessions*. I know I'm no Augustine, and I have no literary pretensions, but I do want *The Wanderer Talks Truth* to be my spiritual testament, my *Confessions*.

My music is all over this book. It is, after all, an important part of who I was—*and who I am*—as a man and as a Christian. So throughout these pages you'll hear familiar songs, and you'll find the familiar faces and voices of my friends and colleagues: Bob Dylan, John Lennon, Lou Reed, Bruce Springsteen, Paul Simon, Dick Clark, Sam Cooke, Bobby Darin, Buddy Holly, Ritchie Valens, the Big Bopper, Waylon Jennings, Van Morrison, Bonnie Raitt, and so many others.

We're all wanderers—they are, and you are, just as I am—and we all want to go home, even when we don't know there's a home waiting for us.

1 BRONX SOUL

IF YOU WANT TO GET to know me—if *I* want to get to know me—we've got to go back to the Bronx.

I'm not talking about the Bronx we can visit today, by taking the expressway or the subway. I'm talking about the Bronx of my childhood, a place of giants and monuments: Yankee Stadium, with its centerfield owned by Joe DiMaggio, and the Bronx Zoo, with its prowling lions.

But let's turn the lens to a tighter focus. I'm not just talking about *the Bronx* of my childhood. I'm talking about the *Belmont* neighborhood, Bronx's "Little Italy." Today it shows up on the short lists of tourist attractions in Manhattan. It's famous for its Italian restaurants. When I was a kid, the eateries were there, and their menus were substantially the same, but it wasn't "cuisine"; it was just normal good food.

We had our own grocer too, with fresh stock of mozzarella floating in big bowls, bushels of basil, bushels of tomatoes, calamari in trays of ice, barrels overflowing with olives—brown, black, red, and every possible shade of green—and salamis and dry cheeses hanging by twine from the rafters. The ceiling fans turned slow and mixed all those aromas together. Whether you were talking about the business or its owner, it made no difference; they were equivalent terms: Joe the Grocer.

We had our funeral parlor that respected our mix of customs from the Old World and the New. We had our candy shop—Moe's, on the corner of 183rd Street and Beaumont. A little storefront, it was stuffed with goodies—Mary Janes and Beeman's and Black Jack Gum, Reed's Hard Candy and Baby Ruth bars. From the day I was old enough to toddle from the front stoop of our apartment building with a nickel in my hand, Moe's was my second home.

We had our record store, and you can bet that *Hit Parade*'s Top Ten were in the front window. Sinatra owned the airwaves the way DiMaggio owned centerfield, and these were points of pride for us in Belmont. We Italian Americans weren't the stereotypical gangsters Hollywood made us out to be. We had arrived. We were just as American as anybody else. What's more, we were shaping America's new attitudes and styles. Now every teenager with a radio was singing like Sinatra. And every kid on every sandlot was rounding third with those long, loping strides like the Yankee Clipper.

The neighborhood grew out of the immigrant waves that washed over Ellis Island from the 1880s through the 1920s. My people arrived sometime in the middle of that. Italian Americans made their own culture. It was transitional. They were eager, but not quite able, to leave behind their old ways. They were anxious to look like Americans but a little resentful of the mainstream American prejudice against Italian immigrants, played out in gangster movies and newsreel and print coverage of Al Capone.

You could see all this at play on the faces of the young (and not-so-young) men who held up the lampposts on our street corners. They wore bluster like a costume covering their frustrations and insecurities. Dangling cigarettes, wearing expensive hats and suit jackets in the oppressive heat of a New York July, they were mafioso wannabes.

Those were just some of the faces in the crowd—and it *was* a crowd—on the sidewalks of Belmont, overflowing onto the stoops and steps, where the older folks gossiped and complained and the younger guys taunted other guys and sang out their love to half the girls who walked by.

Bronx's Little Italy was little, but it packed a lot.

◦ ◦ ◦

In the beginning, my own Bronx was smaller still. It was a two-bedroom, second-story walk-up, rented for thirty-six dollars a month by the most improbably matched couple in Belmont.

My father, Pasquale—my hero in so many ways—was like no one else you ever met. He was a dreamer, with an infinite capacity for wonder and awe. Put him in a museum or a park, and he had all he needed to transport his mind. He could pick up a rock or pull down a leaf, turn it over, and trace the veins as he waxed rapturous on nature's great forces.

He could do the same thing in front of an impressionist masterpiece at the Metropolitan Museum of Art. He had strong opinions. When I was very small, we'd go there or to the Museum of Modern Art, and he'd hold me up so I could see two paintings side by side. "See that one, Dion," he'd say, pointing to the Dalí. "That's the work of a draftsman. It's all mathematics. It's produced."

3

"Now look at this one." Then he'd turn my head so I could see a Van Gogh: "This is expression. The guy couldn't get the paint onto the canvas fast enough to keep pace with his mind."

I don't want to give the impression we were great pals. We weren't. My father was pretty self-absorbed, and he had a violent temper, which often found a convenient object in his only son. He was not above using his son as a shield or decoy when he shoplifted. And unlike most dads, he had *time* to visit parks and museums, because he never held a steady job. In more than ninety years of life on this earth, he never once made enough money to pay taxes.

He hovered around the edges of show business. Pasquale made puppets and gave shows in the resorts in the Catskills. He kept audiences amused between sets of the main event, the musical or comedy acts. Dad drew down forty dollars a night, but the shows were few and far between.

My father was way ahead of the curve on many things. Nutrition and fitness fascinated him, and he was careful about his diet long before it became trendy. He was into health foods, and the staples of his diet were blackstrap molasses, buttermilk, and yogurt. He worked out in his homemade gym in the basement of our building. He cobbled his own weights together by pouring concrete into tomato cans and fitting a bar between them. Again, he could do this because he never held a job.

Somehow this guy persuaded Frances Campanile to marry him.

My mother, Frances, was Pasquale's opposite in every way. She was hardworking, and she hated handouts. Once I asked her what it was like to live in the Great Depression; she answered that she never noticed there was a Depression, because she always had "good jobs." By "good jobs" she meant seamstress work in the sweatshops. But she was happy to have them. She was dutiful about everything. As an employee and as a mother, she did what she was expected to do. If we managed to pay the rent every month—and somehow we did—it's because my mother was working at her "good jobs" and pulling down a regular paycheck. And because she could never abide the shame of an unpaid bill.

They say opposites attract, and my parents would be proof of that. They married in 1936, and they brought me and then my two sisters into that little world called the Bronx.

Opposites may indeed attract. But I can only go by what I see, and I never saw much of the attraction going on. I saw *plenty* of the opposition.

My parents never discussed anything. They argued, and they argued constantly. They yelled about money, mostly, but that was connected to everything else: my father's failure as a provider, my mother's shame and her resentment over the long hours she spent slaving in hat factories. They yelled simultaneously, since each had little interest in what the other had to say, and it had all been said a thousand times anyway. As I got old enough, I raised my own voice and added it to the mix.

Maybe it explains my ability, these many years later, to sing and shout for long, grueling hours at a rock-and-roll show and then do the same thing all over again the next night.

But I'm getting ahead of myself. And I'm not getting to the heart and soul of the Bronx I knew.

✺ ✺ ✺

If you asked me in 1954 what was the heart of my neighborhood, I wouldn't have needed a moment to think. Like any teenage boy, I liked to eat, but my heart didn't race when I gazed into the window at Joe's grocery. It raced like Daytona, though, when I stood at the neighborhood record store, Cousin's, owned by Lou Cicchetti.

I was ten years old the first time I heard Hank Williams sing, and the experience was life-changing. I remember the moment vividly. It was a Sunday, and I could smell supper cooking in the kitchen, my mother's tomato sauce. But when I heard that voice, nothing else mattered to me. For a boy in the Bronx, it was exotic, with its country moan and warble and its southern twang. But this singer was touching on something universal. If you were human, you were already tuned in to his station. I caught his name when the song ended, and the name of the song, too: "I'm So Lonesome I Could Cry."

I bought it at Cousin's the next day, and I started saving my change so I could buy everything else the guy had recorded. The money I used to spend at Moe's candy store now had a new destination. Mr. Cicchetti knew to call me whenever the store got anything new by "that country singer," Hank Williams.

This was right around the time my parents bought me my first guitar. On my instrument and with my voice, I tried to imitate whatever I heard my hero doing on his records. And I must have been pretty good at it, because my father started booking gigs for me. It was cute: a scrawny eleven-year-old in a cowboy hat and kerchief singing "Cold, Cold Heart." By doing what I loved for an hour or two, I could earn enough to pay a month's rent—and still have enough left over to buy a stack of records at Cousin's.

What a time to be alive! And what a time to be drawing down those airwaves! Television had invaded American homes and taken away all the great dramas and comedies from the radio bandwidth—from Sid Caesar to *The Lone Ranger*. Video didn't kill the radio star, but it sure took him off the air when it put him on the screen.

Meanwhile, a new star arose to take the old one's place. It was music, sweet music. With everything else gone over to TV, radio became all music, all the time, with occasional breaks for sports. And the radios themselves got smaller as the tubes inside gave way to transistors. The family radio console used to be the big centerpiece of living room furniture. Now that radios were portable, one kid's favorite disc jockey could become the whole neighborhood's entertainment. All it took was a kid, a radio, and a set of concrete steps by the sidewalk.

I was that kid. And when I wasn't playing my radio, I was playing my guitar.

After school I'd run home to catch the last half-hour of the *Don Larkin Country Show* coming out of Newark, New Jersey. Afterward I'd rush downstairs to the front stoop to sing "Honky Tonk Blues" and "Jambalaya." My friends would ask me, "What's a honky-tonk? What on earth is jambalaya?" I didn't know, but they sure sounded good coming out of my mouth. They were mine somehow, though they weren't like anything I knew in the Belmont neighborhood or anything served in our restaurants. Maybe this was a first taste of transcendence and a hint of salvation.

1 BRONX SOUL

❷ REBELS AND CAUSES

3 MY MUSIC AND MY MUSE

THEY SAY THAT INFANTS HAVE a drive to bond with the family and stay close to home.

Teenagers go the other way: Their drive is to define themselves apart from the family. They're beginning the process of detachment that, in a healthy kid, leads to a gradual separation and then adulthood.

I wasn't what you'd call a healthy kid. When I was a teenager, my drive for independence was stuck in overdrive. Maybe my circumstances aggravated what otherwise might have been an ordinary case of adolescent rebellion. But our home wasn't happy, and I didn't really want to be there. I had a better time on the streets, where I didn't have to listen to anybody yelling. So I went out; and as much as I could, I stayed out. And I did what too many troubled kids do when they're out on the streets all the time.

I don't blame my environment, because I made the choices. There were kids on my block, kids in my grade, kids with less-than-optimal home situations, who chose to study anyway, and they did well in life. I made my own choices, and many of them were bad.

Maybe most teenagers feel like awkward misfits, but I felt that I was the only one without a place. I wasn't an athlete, wasn't a scholar. I didn't want to be home. So I joined a gang, the Daggers, and we made mischief, mostly misdemeanors—petty theft, vandalism, brawling, and protecting our "turf" from the gangs in the neighborhoods nearby. If you've ever seen *West Side Story*, you know what I mean. That was a Gucci rendition of what we were doing. (We didn't choreograph our rumbles.)

Even in the gangs I didn't feel like I fit. But the rebellion seemed to answer to some hunger I had. I wanted to overturn the whole thing—our miserable home, the Italian American scene with all its insecurity and posturing. Violence and vandalism answered my need to rebel. Think of the teenage Augustine stealing pears from his neighbor for no good reason. They tasted lousy. He was rebelling as I was rebelling. We were doing it because it was wrong, because it upset the order of things. To us in the Bronx, James Dean was a lightweight, though he was cool in *Rebel Without a Cause*.

When I got dressed in the morning, I went for the "rebel king" look: black leather jacket, T-shirt, blue jeans, Cuban heels, and Garrison belt. I slicked my hair back on the sides but liked to let my curls go wild up top.

Once when I was strutting down Belmont, someone called out to me, "Hey, Dion!"

I knew the voice. It was the pastor of Our Lady of Mount Carmel Parish, Msgr. Pernicone. I returned his greeting in some hip way.

He kept going: "Dion, what's this movie, *Rebel Without a Cause*?"

I explained about the film and about James Dean and the coolness of it all.

Monsignor was unimpressed. "Dion, why rebel without a cause? Rebel for the truth, and you got something."

Monsignor was one of the few people who could get away with talking to me that way. It wasn't that I was religious. I wasn't, and neither was anyone in my family. We had all been baptized Catholics, but there was no evidence of it in our homes—no crucifix or picture of the Blessed Mother anywhere. If we DiMuccis owned a Bible, I never knew about it. We went to church only for weddings and funerals. When my father talked about nature, he seemed to assume that the world's design required a Designer—"God made it that way"—but that's as far as I heard him go. My grandmother, my father's mother, was a devout believer and a daily communicant. Whenever she greeted me, she would look up to heaven and thank God for my existence. But she didn't say anything more about it; and I wasn't particularly interested anyway.

Msgr. Pernicone, though—he was different. He commanded respect, not because of his title or because of his priestly robes but because he was the real deal, and everybody knew it. He looked over Belmont like he was its father, and I guess he was, in a spiritual sense.

Born in Sicily in 1903, Joseph Maria Pernicone was ordained for the Archdiocese of New York in 1926, and his first assignment out of the box was to Mount Carmel in the Bronx. In the thirties he got transferred to Poughkeepsie, but he came back as our pastor when I was four years old. The history of the parish records the first words of his comeback sermon: "As your pastor, I have but one aim, one purpose, one desire: to serve your immortal souls."

And, man, did he do it. The guy used to stand out in front of the huge doors of the church and call out to people as they went by. He would call them over and ask after their families. He would keep up with their problems and successes. There were thousands of Italian Americans registered in that parish when I was a kid, and he seemed to know them all.

"Yo, Dion," he'd call out to me from his place by the door. "Come over here."

Only he could summon me like that. I may have gone over slowly, but I went.

"Dion, what makes a man happy?"

Man, I gave him a list. There was a cute redhead who had moved into the neighborhood; a date with her would make me happy. Owning a T-Bird, that would make me happy. A Gibson guitar.

"No, Dion. You got it all wrong. The virtuous man is a happy man." Then he cited his source: "St. Thomas Aquinas."

"Yeah, yeah," I'd say as I started walking away. What I was thinking was, "What the hell is virtue?"

So I'd call out to him: "Monsignor, what's virtue?"

All these years later I can still recite his reply from memory: "Virtue is the habitual and firm disposition to do the good." I've never forgotten the definition, even if I've never lived up to it very well.

Monsignor had been at Mount Carmel long before I was born. He would be there long after I left. He built our parochial school.

He had a tough mind, and he wasn't afraid to use it. He held a doctorate in canon law, but he didn't flash it to impress you. He stood on those steps and looked around, and he saw forty thousand "immortal souls" for whom Almighty God would hold him accountable. He was going to be a father to them, whether or not they disowned the Church.

Even hipsters noticed that. Some of my buddies played baseball, and sometimes their games were on Sunday. Msgr. Pernicone would add a special game-day Mass to the schedule, early in the morning, and then he'd call the opposing team and invite them as well.

If Cousin's record store was the heart of my Belmont, Mount Carmel was the soul, embodied for me and everybody else in Joseph Pernicone.

When I was fourteen he was made an auxiliary bishop of the archdiocese, and we had a big celebration in the neighborhood. By then I was performing regularly in the local bars and restaurants, so the folks at the parish, during a momentary lapse of reason, asked me to show up and play him a song.

Cutup that I was, I picked a popular country tune popularized by Johnnie Scott:

> Hey Joe!
> Where'd you find that pearly-girly?
> Where'd you get that jolly-dolly?
> How'd you rate that dish I wish was mine?[1]

Next day it didn't matter that Monsignor was now a bishop. It didn't matter that I had sung a totally inappropriate song at his party. The man had a sense of humor and a strong sense of who he was and what he was about. Next day he was back on the front steps.

"Hey, Dion! What's prudence?"

"Prudence? Is that like prunes?"

And we were off on another twenty-minute conversation.

If you asked me back then, I would have dismissed Monsignor as a local "character." My buddies would cross the street rather than risk his summons, but I regularly put myself in conversation's way. Maybe it was part of my all-out rebellion, but I liked arguing with him. He gave it to you straight, but he listened to you and took you seriously, and then he was right back at you. I liked to *think* I was tough. But I *knew* that man was strong. One day I would learn the difference between strong and tough.

I had a similar relationship with a social worker in our neighborhood, Sarah Alba. She was assigned, like the kindly social worker in *West Side Story*, to encourage us young thugs to move on from gangs to goodness. Sarah was young, probably just out of college, and very intelligent; and she obviously cared passionately about what she was doing. She didn't hesitate to bring religious faith into our discussions, to ground our morality.

For some reason I felt threatened by Sarah in a way I was by nobody else. She got my blood boiling more than any member of an opposing gang, even if he were approaching me with a knife. If she was right, I was very wrong—in fact, I was a failure —and it frustrated me that I couldn't pull together an intelligent response to her.

So I openly mocked her, especially if my friends were around to hear it. I called her "stupid." She never seemed concerned or bothered. She just kept putting the truth in front of us. If we wanted to be treated with respect, we should treat others with respect. If we wanted to enjoy the benefits of a just society, we should behave justly.

Sarah was obviously happy, and she was free in a way we were not—and this galled me. Worst of all, she had faith in me. I watched her, day after day, listened to her, waiting for her to slip up in her logic so I could make a fool of her. She never did.

What I saw in her was what I saw in Monsignor. I didn't recognize it then for what it was, but I do now. It was integrity. It was virtue. It was the love of God. It was the joy of living, in the flesh of my neighborhood.

But again, I didn't recognize it at the time.

A funny thing about the urge to rebel and be different: It drove us guys into gangs where we pretty much all talked and dressed and wiped our noses the same way. I found myself in rebellion against that, too. So I switched my allegiance from the Daggers to the Fordham Baldies, another local gang, named after the American bald eagle. It didn't help matters.

The street was like a church, with its own sacraments, rites of passage, and obligations. I started getting drunk when I was twelve, smoking pot when I was thirteen, and shooting heroin when I was fourteen.

Gang life began to have real casualties. My friends started to disappear—to prison, to overdose, or to knife wounds. At least for the funerals I got to church.

I felt a little better when I was stoned—I could forget and drop into oblivion—but I still hadn't found the place where I fit. Home didn't feel like home, but neither did the gang or the street.

"Dion, what makes a man happy?" I'd already heard the answer, but I wasn't listening.

3 MY MUSIC AND MY MUSE

SO YOU KNOW BY NOW that I've always had a taste for the exotic. Why else would an Italian boy in the Bronx be moaning a country blues song about a lonesome whistle blown down South? And you know by now that I had a drive to set myself apart, to transcend the place where I found myself, whether in our angry apartment or on the mean streets.

Well, you can imagine the alarms that went off in my brain the first day I saw the new girl in Belmont: Susan Butterfield. With a name like that, with her flaming auburn hair and her freckles, she stood out among the dark-haired Italians. Don't get me wrong: The neighborhood girls were gorgeous, but Susan Butterfield was beyond gorgeous. She was exotic, transcendent. Talking to her only confirmed this. She had a deadpan wit—delivered in a kind of understated monotone —and an inner toughness that I could only envy. I had met my match.

This was like nothing I had known before. It's like nothing I've known since. I was fifteen, and I knew suddenly that *home* was what I wanted (though not the home I already had), and that Susan would be my home.

17

But how to talk *her* into that idea? That was the question.

My break came when Susan's all-girls school invited me to be an instrumental accompanist for their big play. There was a campfire scene that required a guitar to be strumming in the background, but they didn't have a single guitarist enrolled in the entire school. So they had to bring in a boy, and by this time everybody in the neighborhood equated guitar with Dion DiMucci. (Remember my inglorious serenade for Msgr. Pernicone?)

So I played. I was more diligent and prompt in showing up for those rehearsals than I'd ever been for anything at my schools. When I was playing I was playing to her, trying to catch her beautiful glance.

And I caught it. I caught it! She could make me laugh without ever cracking a smile. She could wither me to nothing with just the arch of an eyebrow. She could play her funny monotone and deadpan the way a virtuoso plays a fine instrument. (If you want to know about my end of it, listen to a little song I eventually recorded called "Wonderful Girl.")

Something was happening to me. Many decades later I would come across these words of a medieval mystic: "Love is an eye, and to love is to see." *Wow*, isn't that the truth!

When I met Susan it was as if I saw everything around me for the first time. Before, it was all like a Picasso painting—helter-skelter, disjointed, and out of proportion. Now everything was ordered toward her. Suddenly my inner drive wasn't about overturning everything in my lousy world. It wasn't about rebelling. I wanted to build something. I wanted to build up a life and build it with Susan.

I don't remember a particular moment when everything changed, but in retrospect I see the signs.

One afternoon I wandered into a bookshop and spent maybe an hour in the art section. (My father's tours through the museums got me hooked for life.) I wanted to buy every fat volume on the shelves and spend hours poring over their brilliant colors. I walked out with books on Picasso, Cezanne, Renoir, Modigliani, and Monet. Over the next few days I filled my head with those reproductions—visions, really, they were so beautiful. But at the end of my reading, one small image stayed with me, and it wasn't even a painting. It was a black-and-white photograph of the elderly Claude Monet, looking patriarchal, a portly man with a vast expanse of gray beard, seated in some kind of lawn chair and surrounded by a multitude of children and grandchildren.

That's me, I thought. *That's who I want to be.*

Maybe I'd found a new way to be a rebel—with a cause, this time, and that cause had a name: Susan.

* * *

But what did I know about loving a girl?

I knew one thing for sure: I didn't want, ever, to have the kind of relationship my parents had. I didn't want the fighting and yelling and constant one-upping with putdowns.

Knowing what you *don't* want is easy, but it only gets you so far.

So I'll say it again: Where was a guy like me—a brute from the Bronx—going to learn about love?

Well, it's funny the kind of knowledge you can pick up on the street.

I know what you're thinking, and that's not what I mean. I'm not talking about dirty jokes or dirty magazines or nighttime hookups in Crotona Park. There was plenty of that in my crowd, but it didn't teach me anything of value. I'm talking about the most valuable lesson I ever learned about love.

One afternoon I was doing my usual thing, which was nothing. This time I was sitting by those steps at Mount Carmel Church. Not far away stood Msgr. Pernicone, holding court as usual, watching over his people as they passed by. For some reason he wasn't interested in quizzing me on the virtues that day. I could enjoy the moment in peace.

Time passed, and people stopped to greet him and complain to him about their spouses or kids or the world in general. Sometimes they'd do it in rapid Italian, sometimes in English, and sometimes in a mix of both. In the end they'd say something inconclusive, throw up their hands, give Monsignor an affectionate good-bye, and then go their way. The world turned slowly. I half listened.

Then something different happened. A young couple, husband and wife, maybe twenty-five years old, approached Monsignor. The husband was walking with a firm purpose and a lot of attitude, his lips closed tight as he pulled his wife along. I knew right away that this conversation wasn't going to be like the others.

The guy had hardly stopped at Monsignor's side when he said, "Father, we're gonna get divorced. I don't love her anymore." You can bet he was saying this to the very priest who had administered the vows and offered the Mass at their wedding.

Monsignor didn't hesitate. He hardly blinked. He said to the guy, "Well then, love her."

The guy couldn't have been more baffled if Monsignor had responded in Japanese. "What are you talking about? Didn't you hear me? I just said we're gonna get divorced *because I don't love her anymore!*"

The priest just stood stock-still and said it again: "Well then, love her."

The guy was obviously getting frustrated. "Uh, Father, can you hear me? I said, I DON'T LOVE HER ANYMORE!" And he was shouting by now, so everybody on the street heard him.

Monsignor just kept his cool: "I don't think *you* heard what *I* said. I said, 'Then love her.' *Love* is a verb before it's a noun. It's an action, and it's a decision. It's something you *will* to do. It's not just something you feel."

God can do anything. He can take my afternoon laziness and some hotshot's selfishness, throw them together, and it comes out as a three-credit course on true love.

That conversation stuck with me. I remembered it a thousand times in the decade to come, even in moments when I was far from God, far from the gospel, and years from my last sober moment. *Love is not just something you feel.*

❖ ❖ ❖

Still, I was feeling it at fifteen. I was feeling it and singing it. Susan became a focus even for my music. It wasn't just an escape for me now. It was a way of building a life.

I didn't want to end up like my father. I had seen my uncles laugh up their sleeves at him. They thought he was a loser, a failure, a good-for-nothing; and they told him so, often, with his whole family in earshot. They had contempt for my father, and we were ashamed—my mom, my sisters, and me. We all came to scorn him too.

Music was my assurance that I wouldn't grow up to be like Pasquale DiMucci, the failed puppeteer. It was something I could do better than anybody else in my neighborhood, which is the same as saying "my world." I could be good for something. In fact, I could be the best at something. I would show my uncles and my mother, for sure, but most of all I would show Susan.

It all started in fun though. On Fridays I played "professionally"—for tips—at a place called Ermondo's. It wasn't a bad gig. Every now and then you'd get some guy in the mob who wanted to impress his girl, so he'd make a big show of dropping twenty bucks in your hat. In 1954 that was money.

The hottest music, though, wasn't in the bar. It was out on the streets. In New York there was a long tradition of street singing. In the years that coincided with my adolescence, this developed into a beautiful art form.

Groups of guys would try to outdo one another with their intricate harmonies. And since we usually didn't have instruments, we'd try to imitate instrumental sounds with our voices. That's the origin of the style of music known as *doo-wop*. At night my friends and I would take the train to Harlem's Apollo Theater to hear the hottest bands, and all the way home we'd sing the songs we had just heard, using those nonsense syllables as filler and backup. Who needed instruments?

We did the same thing when we worked up original songs. We belted out variations on "I love you," and we surrounded them with a big band's worth of vocal accompaniment—rhythmically syncopated, harmonically sophisticated. Much of it was improvised, but over time it got polished to a high luster. Who needed words?

Of course, there were other reasons we stuck to "I love you" and nonsense syllables. I sometimes joke that, in our entire gang, we probably didn't have enough functioning brain cells to write a coherent set of lyrics. So *dit-didit-didit-didit doo-wa* would have to do.

Doo-wop singing got popular, and it got competitive. The singing groups talked about their rivalries as seriously as the gangs did! As I walked around the Bronx, I took note of who was putting out the best sound. Three guys especially impressed me: Carlo Mastrangelo, Fred Milano, and Angelo D'Aleo.

In fact, as doo-wop began to occupy the radio airwaves, it was clear that Carlo, Fred, and Angelo were better than anybody else doing the job. Anywhere.

Doo-wop ruled the airwaves, and we were singing it on the streets of New York, the media capital of the world. Someone was bound to notice. I can't say I expected it to happen, but neither was I surprised when it did.

※ ※ ※

When I held Susan, when I held a guitar, when I held a high note, I felt like I had nothing to fear. I was the guy in control of my life and my future.

Sure, my self-confidence leaned a little on the stuff I was pumping into my bloodstream. But that was OK. I was in control of that, too. I could handle my liquor. And I wasn't using heroin every day, just when I needed something special or a booster shot.

I could look at myself in a mirror and tell myself that I wasn't a drunk or a junkie. I wasn't a creepy addict like you saw in the

23

movies. And I knew those guys. I saw them lying in the alleyways. But that wasn't me.

I was master of my destiny, with Susan on my arm and audiences enthralled.

4 A CHOSEN FEW

I'd never have acknowledged it back in those days, but there were many things I respected about my father: his artistic sense, his independence, his intellectual curiosity, and—in a strange way—his defiance. My uncles were right about wanting my father to get a job; but I admired him for not caring what others thought about him. My mother and sisters and I suffered from his defiance of social norms and family expectations. But there was something attractive about his self-confidence. He was a rebel, and he had a cause, of sorts, in himself. He pursued a certain vision of leisure and ease, and he didn't care what anybody thought about it. (I learned much later that defiance is not a bad disposition if it can be turned toward the right kind of goals.)

In a moment of weakness, I guess, I agreed to do an audition my father had wangled with Bob and Gene Schwartz of the newly formed Mohawk Records. I packed my guitar and took the Third Avenue el to their offices downtown on West Fifty-Fourth Street. I gave it my best. I played "Boppin' the Blues," a song I used to rock the church dances.

Well, there's something to be said for meaning what you're singing. I had already had enough experience performing. I knew how to read an audience. And it was obvious from their expressions that the Schwartz brothers liked what I had. Gene sat me down and told me they had a song ready-made for me—something called "The Chosen Few." They started to roll the tape.

Ugh. What else can I say? I didn't like it at all. It was too stiff, too smarmy. It could have come off an assembly line. The orchestration was way too much, yet even the orchestra was overwhelmed by a melodramatic harp playing sad, sad arpeggios.

I told the Schwartz brothers what I thought.

They said they didn't care. "Cut it anyway."

So I said I would. I was a seventeen-year-old with a recording contract. It didn't matter that I'd signed with a fledgling record label. It didn't matter that I disliked the song. I'd give it a shot. I was a *recording artist*.

We pressed "The Chosen Few" with another gem as its B-side. This one was called "Out in Colorado." It was a cowboy tune, from the same school as "Oh, What a Beautiful Morning"—but no grit in it, just *nice*. In my world, *nice* was the kiss of death.

But I was a long way from my street corner in Belmont.

٭ ٭ ٭

God bless Bob and Gene Schwartz. Maybe they didn't have good music in those cans, but they knew they had a hit, and they were right. "The Chosen Few" scored in Boston. It soared in Boston, which is a very important market. Pretty soon demand was so great that Bob and Gene couldn't keep up. So they arranged to issue the single on the better-known Jubilee label, for wider distribution. Mohawk Records had made an impressive debut. So had I.

And guess what? "The Chosen Few" sold pretty briskly at Cousin's shop in Belmont. I was temporarily a hero to the gang, to my parents, to Joe the grocer, everybody. I can't say for sure, but I'll bet even Msgr. Pernicone was pleased. That doesn't mean they were uncritical. In fact, most of the neighbors—and even my parents—were eager to tell me that I sounded better on the street than on plastic.

It didn't matter. I was set.

I quit school. Why bother with it? It could only get in the way of my career. I had work, money, respect—and Susan. I didn't need anything else.

The Schwartzes began to talk about a follow-up. I didn't want to do it with the invisible fogies from the last record. And I figured I had a little bit of leverage, now that I'd scored a solid regional hit for Mohawk. So I told Gene I would rather not work with their in-house vocalists. I could put together a better group from the Bronx. He laughed, but he was willing to indulge me.

I hurried home and rounded up the best I knew from the neighborhoods nearby: Carlo and Freddy from Mapes Avenue, Angelo from Tremont. The first time we all sang together, we were just improvising to a tune called "I Wonder Why," but it was like we were in ecstasy. The singing was inspired. Each of us was following a different vocal line—spontaneously—but they all blended perfectly, the harmonies and the rhythms. I thought I had found the key to heaven. The sound was so strong. I had never before felt like I was *inside* a song the way I was when I sang with those guys.

We took our act to the street and added more tunes. When we sang "That's My Desire," the neighbors went crazy. I knew I had found the combination.

I knew we needed a name, and I wanted to find one that could serve equally well for a bowling team or a rock-and-roll group. I decided to call us simply "Dion and the Belmonts"—because when we sang on Belmont Avenue, we owned the place.

We went to Gene Schwartz and sang our stuff, just like we were on the street, and the effect was the same as always. If I close my eyes, I can still see the man grinning as we sang.

Mohawk could put away its harps and choirs and orchestras. The act now was Dion and the Belmonts.

We knew what we had was magic. We had the sound. When we sang on the street, the music was like an electrical current running through the crowd that gathered around us.

We couldn't wait to get it onto plastic. It never occurred to us to worry. We had crazy confidence. But we had earned it.

And were we ever loose in the studio! The guys thought it was a lark. They figured it couldn't last, so they were just going to enjoy it. I was a lot more driven, more intense, and I planned to make a life of it. So I took to scheduling rehearsals—and dragging the guys out of bed when they didn't show up. The music was worth it.

It was certainly worth a lot to Bob and Gene, who were now pretty heavily invested in their boys from the Bronx. Gene worried about our diet and what spicy foods might do to our voices. We thought he was hilarious. We were good, and young, and indestructible.

With my drive the work got done. With the guys' humor it stayed fun. With the Schwartzes' savvy we went national.

In the early months of 1958, there was hardly a soul with a radio that didn't know our explosive hit "I Wonder Why," which peaked at number twenty-two on the U.S. charts and had a ten-week run on *Billboard*'s Top Twenty.

> I wonder why
> I love you like I do.
> Is it because I think you love me too?
> I wonder why
> I love you like I do,
> like I do.
> I told my friends
> that we would never part.
> They often said
> that you would break my heart.
> I wonder why
> they think that we will part
> we will part.
> When you're with me
> I'm sure you're always true.
> When I'm away
> I wonder what you do.
> I wonder why
> I'm sure you're always true,
> always true....
> Don't know why I do.[1]

The lyrics couldn't be simpler. There's no word over two syllables, and most of them have only one. But the emotions are complex. We sang teenage feelings in teenage words that reflected real teen emotion. It's a profession of love but also a confession of uncertainty, insecurity. When that guy said, "I wonder why," he was really *wondering*, and he was more than a little afraid. We could sing it because we all had felt it. Listeners, for their part, knew it when they heard it.

Still, it takes more than poetry to make a hit, and we threw everything we had at that song. Carlo's long, stuttering opening was epoch-making in doo-wop. The session musicians were the best. They were actually the guys we'd been paying to hear at the Apollo Theater throughout our teen years. The harmonies, from start to finish, were as good as anything we'd ever done on the street.

Another thrill for me was the B-side, "Teen Angel," which was my first crack at songwriting.

We followed strong in 1958, with two more Top Forty hits, "No One Knows" and "Don't Pity Me."

* * *

I wasn't yet twenty years old, and I was already a millionaire a couple times over. It happened that fast. As I write this in the year 2010, that still seems like a lot of money. In 1958 it was truly a fortune, and not a small one.

I drank the good stuff. I wore nice clothes. I bought myself a Thunderbird. I signed a lease on a big apartment in Manhattan, and I stuffed it full of the latest designs in furniture. (I wanted to impress Susan.)

But I still had a good bit of my mother in me. I was never able to indulge the usual rock-star excesses. I didn't need seven cars; I could only drive one at a time. So I bought only one. I didn't need seven apartments; I could only live in one at a time. So I got one. I didn't need to drink the good stuff out of antique crystal. It served its purpose in any cup.

I didn't mind showing off, but I couldn't bring myself to spend freely. So even though I was pouring money away on my addictions, I was still socking a lot away in the bank. Like my mother, I was making sure the bills were paid.

And I made sure *her* bills were paid. One thing I was able to do now was remove the stigma of poverty and malingering that my father had brought on our household. My mother could be proud of something—because she could be proud of me. I moved Mom and Dad and the girls out to a house in the suburbs, and now I paid their rent, and it always got paid on time.

5 MAKING NEW RULES

ROCK AND ROLL, THE ETERNAL youth, was just a toddler in 1958. And like most toddlers, it had plenty of self-confidence, no real experience to draw from, and no clear understanding of the rules.

Confidence? Listen to what Danny and the Juniors were singing that year: "Rock and roll will always be.... It'll go down in history." It's the sense of permanence that comes with money and fame. The young people were buying what we put on offer, and the audience was growing. What's more, the fans were *young*, so they were likely to be around for a long time.

As for experience, there was none to have. Nowadays Ivy League universities have endowed professorships for rock-and-roll historians. Back then rock and roll had no history. Most kitchen cupboards had canned goods that were older than rock music.

From this distance we can now see that many powerful forces were coming together. The country had a lot of confidence. We'd won a big war. We had some money—we were manufacturing everything and exporting it to the rest of the bombed-out

33

world. Radio had brought us together as a nation in a way we'd never experienced before; then TV hit the gas pedal on that process. American prosperity gave the country's young people a lot of disposable income, making "youth culture" possible for the first time. Marketers and admen were just beginning to figure out how to manipulate this enormous opportunity.

Of course, none of us could see it then. We were just kids having a good time, and we fell into a barrel of money.

The rules? We were making the rules.

The Schwartz brothers had good business sense. They knew that personal appearances sold records. If the kids heard your song on the radio, they might like it. But if they *saw* you in concert—or even on television—they were more likely to bond with you and buy more of your music. They booked us on long tours of successive one-night stands, and we loved it. The audiences energized us.

We also did TV, including ABC's new *daily* showcase of rock and roll, *American Bandstand*, with its young host, Dick Clark.

Dick wasn't a whole lot older than I was, but he was plenty more grown-up. He was a shrewd businessman, and he knew that his job was as much about wooing parents as winning teens. He was the wholesome face the entertainment industry put on rock and roll—this sexually suggestive, interracial, boundary-smashing phenomenon.

Dick's own rise was meteoric. Just a year or so before I appeared on his national show, he had been a disc jockey in Philadelphia. Now he had millions of Americans watching him after school, every single day, Monday through Friday, for half an hour. Those kids spent more time with Dick Clark than they spent in civics class.

I can't say I established myself as a budding TV star. When Dion and the Belmonts showed up to sing "I Wonder Why" on *Bandstand* Dick focused on me as the front man. I was so nervous and so painfully shy that he not only asked the questions but had to answer them as well, because all I could do was gulp and shrug. There was stark terror in his eyes. And he wasn't half as scared as I was.

Rock and roll was bringing people together, and I'm not just talking about couples on the dance floor. *Bandstand* had wide appeal, thanks to Dick Clark; and the show had universal reach, thanks to network television. Daily exposure drove the message home. And the message, again in the words of Danny and the Juniors, was "Rock and roll is here to stay."

Bandstand also ensured that rock meant the same thing to kids in California and kids in New Jersey. Everybody was grooving to the same bands; and as long as one of them was Dion and the Belmonts, I was happy.

It's funny, but Dick Clark was almost like a secular pastor to me—a father figure. He tried, in a manner similar to Msgr. Pernicone's, to teach me important life lessons. He must have looked at me in 1958 and wondered whether I could handle the kind of success that was coming my way, especially after he saw his audience in Philly go wild for our group.

I'll never forget what he told me off-camera that day. He told me that fame had given me more authority with kids than any of their teachers had, so I should be very careful of the choices I made. People would believe whatever I said, just because I was their favorite singer. If I said a certain kind of hairstyle made girls look pretty, girls would run out and get it, and their boyfriends would want them to. If I said I liked a particular make and model of automobile, it would become the cool car to have. Dick Clark wanted me to know the perennial message of the *Spiderman* comics: With great power comes great responsibility; with great freedom comes great responsibility.

Dick used his authority wisely and well—for his own gain, yes, but also for the common good. He was honest, reliable, and consistent. Under his direction *Bandstand* helped unite not only regions but also races. Dick hosted both black and white artists on his show, at a time when few people would dare to do so.

I've often said that our songs were black music filtered through an Italian neighborhood in the Bronx. We picked up the basic sounds at the Apollo Theater in Harlem; then we made them our own. Radio's audience was color-blind. They really didn't care about race, as long as you were good. I felt the same way. My thing was to make music that just couldn't be denied. I can't tell you how many times we sang "I Wonder Why" and watched people's surprise as they learned that their favorite song was sung by white guys.

In those early years we often found ourselves on the same bill as Sam Cooke. A preacher's kid, he had recently made the jump from gospel to pop, and his stunning love song, "You Send Me," reached number one in 1957. It was the first of a long string of hits that would include "Only Sixteen," "Chain Gang," "Wonderful World," "Another Saturday Night," and "Twisting the Night Away."

Sam's voice was like King Midas's touch on a melody. He always worked with good material, but it was his interpretation that turned the merely good into gold records.

With any other guy I might be envious and wish him a case of tonsillitis. But Sam was such a gentleman. He was intelligent and struck me as well educated. He was a deeply spiritual man, and one of the few rockers in those years who would casually talk about the Lord in conversation on the tour bus. He seemed to stay close to his gospel roots and his Baptist upbringing.

I got to know him as we traveled, and I got to see his life as grace under pressure. I was really unprepared for what I saw as our tour bus headed south. Sam was the headliner in our show, and people were driving hundreds of miles and spending good money just for the chance to hear him sing. Yet he couldn't stay in the same hotel as his white road crew! He couldn't eat with any of us.

Don't get me wrong. I'm not saying there was no racism in the Bronx when I was growing up. There was hostility toward people from *Brooklyn*, never mind toward non-Italians and nonwhites. But nothing in my upbringing had prepared me for my experience of Jim Crow.

Sam took it all with Christian dignity. He didn't grow moody or cut back on his kindness. He didn't love me any less because I was the same color as the people who were treating him like an animal. In fact, he didn't treat them unkindly either. And racism can cut both ways. It turned on us white singers several times as we traveled, as we walked the Southern city streets late at night, and each time Sam came forward to protect us.

Sam died young, in 1964, the year he charted with "A Change Is Gonna Come." For the change that did come, we can give some of the credit, I believe, to rock and roll.

Some people act like rock and roll is the great savior of mankind. I'm here to tell you it's not. Somebody Else locked up that job a couple thousand years ago.

Other people act like rock and roll is the great Satan. It's not.

Rock and roll is something powerful but morally neutral in itself, like electricity or the automobile. Are those good things? It depends on what you're doing with them.

Dick Clark and Sam Cooke—and lots of other guys—recognized the power they'd been given, and they put it to good use. They made people's lives happier through entertainment. They also made the world a little better through the responsible use of the *authority* their talent had earned for them. They were mentors to me, and examples I'm still trying to follow. Remember Monsignor's definition of virtue: "the habitual and firm disposition to do the good." These guys had a piece of that.

6 THE DAY THE MUSIC WAS BORN

ON THOSE TOURS IN 1958, we went from glory to glory, headlining with the likes of Eddie Cochran ("Summertime Blues"), Gene Vincent ("Be-Bop-A-Lula"), and Bobby Darin ("Splish Splash").

Bobby was another Italian boy from the Bronx, a few years my senior and more hip to the ways of the business world. He became a close friend and a mentor, giving me good advice about how to read my contracts and file my taxes. Bobby grew up the same way I did and had many of the same worries. He spoke to my frugal nature, my inner Mom. A lot of early rockers got jerked around and bled dry by their agents, their record companies, and the crowd of scammers that follow the money wherever it goes. If I managed to survive rock stardom with a couple nickels to rub together, no small credit goes to Bobby Darin, who spoke my language (Bronx) and gave me free accounting lessons on the tour bus.

Glory to glory—in the fall we got invited to join another superstar, Buddy Holly, on what was billed as "The Biggest Show of Stars." Buddy had a streak of hits that could make Joe

DiMaggio jealous: "That'll Be the Day," "Peggy Sue," "Everyday," "Oh, Boy," "Maybe, Baby," and "It's So Easy (to Fall in Love)." He'd only been recording for a year, but he had already established a rock-and-roll sound that everyone was mimicking.

I got to know Buddy when he moved to New York in August. He'd just married a New Yorker, Maria Elena Santiago, and he was happy in his new apartment. (He'd proposed to Maria Elena on their first date.)

We spent three weeks together on "The Biggest Show of Stars," and we established a strong relationship—friendship and mutual musical admiration. When Buddy invited me to join him on his upcoming all-star "Winter Dance Party" tour, I was honored, and I didn't hesitate to say yes.

Now, keep in mind all those things I told you about the early days of rock and roll. There was lots of money flying around, and we were pulling down a good bit of it. But we were nowhere near the days when rock stars owned private jets and traveled with an entourage of valets and hairdressers. Most of the time we went from town to town in the kind of yellow bus we had ridden to school only a few years before. We did our own laundry. We packed our own bags. (I still do. Old habits die hard.)

And we weren't playing big arenas with lighted mirrors in the dressing rooms. We sang our hearts out in venues like Sans Souci Park in Wilkes-Barre, Pennsylvania, where we had to compete for attention with the roller coaster and Ferris wheel.

So when Angelo, Carlo, Freddie, and I signed up for a touring "Party" set for the Midwestern states in the dead of winter, we knew we weren't going on a pleasure cruise. But we could rock and roll with the world's greatest names. Buddy had booked Ritchie Valens—the Latino kid from Los Angeles who'd made it big with "La Bamba"—and the Big Bopper, J.P. Richardson, who was best known for "Chantilly Lace."

You may already know how this story ends; it's part of rock-and-roll mythology. People call February 2, 1959, "the day the music died," after Don McLean's poetic midrash in his 1971 hit "American Pie."

But what you *think* you know may not be the truth. I was there. I was one of the headliners on that concert tour, and I've read all the interviews, all the things that pass themselves off as histories—and I can authoritatively say to you that most of it is bunk. The events, as they happened, have been completely eclipsed by urban legends, cinematic retellings, gossip, and outright grandstanding.

There are people whose lives peaked because they were somewhere near the epicenter of the pop-culture earthquake that happened on February 2, 1959. They've exaggerated their role, which is understandable and forgivable; but in doing so they've distorted history, and they've unintentionally done an injustice to the memory of my friends.

For fifty years I kept quiet about this, until very recently, when the historians at the Rock and Roll Hall of Fame asked me to help them reconcile conflicting accounts of the tour. I gave them the same facts I'm giving you in this book.

I have nothing to lose or gain from my telling of the story. My career was well established when I set out from New York with my group, the Belmonts. That's why we were on an all-star tour in the first place. I've been able, thank God, to continue making music ever since. I never needed to hitch my wagon to a death-star to hold on to fame. I'm willing to bet that most of the people who've come to my shows and bought my records know nothing about my connection with the Winter Dance Party or its fateful events.

Nevertheless, for my friends' sake, I feel obligated to set the record straight.

❉ ❉ ❉

We expected discomfort, but we weren't quite ready for what we got on this three-week "Party." America's heartland is a lovely place full of lovely people; but let me tell you, its winters make New York December look like Palm Beach in May. We made our way through Iowa, where the temperature dropped to twenty-five below zero at high noon. And that's before wind chill.

That would have been all right. We had no desire—and no time—to get out and throw a football around. We would have been happy to sleep on the bus, except that it wasn't the latest model. It was pretty drafty, and its heating system was non-functional.

You think I'm exaggerating? Buddy's drummer on that tour, Carl Bunch, got a nasty case of frostbite while he was sitting on the bus, and he had to be admitted to a local hospital. Buddy wasn't traveling with his band, the Crickets, at the time; they'd had a rift. So we were all sharing backup musicians—and we were all playing backup for one another. Carlo Mastrangelo took over behind the drum kit when Buddy was singing. Ritchie Valens took over the drumming for the Bopper. And Buddy drummed for me. I'm the only rock singer who can boast that Buddy Holly drummed for my backup band.

On the bus we would sing together to keep warm. I wrote us a song called "I'm Gonna Hug My Radiator When I Hit My Hotel Room," and all the guys sang it with gusto. (I recorded it, decades later, on my *Deja Nu* album.)

The schedule got more crowded as the promoters called us with new bookings, new dates, in out-of-the-way places. That meant more time on the road, in the bus. One of those last-minute additions was a show at the Surf Ballroom in Clear Lake, Iowa. By the time we got there, we were all pretty miserable.

Buddy gathered up the headliners and told us he couldn't take another night on the bus; he was going to try to charter a plane to take us to the next stop on the tour, Moorhead, Minnesota. He found a single-engine craft that could seat three in addition to the pilot. The problem was that there were four headliners—Buddy, Ritchie, the Big Bopper, and me. Someone would have to ride the bus.

In a closed dressing room, we flipped a coin to see who was going to fly. The Big Bopper and I won the toss. Buddy would also fly, of course, since he had found the plane.

Then Buddy told us what the flight would cost: $36. Thirty-six bucks. That figure set off an alarm in my brain.

All my childhood I had listened to my parents argue about money and argue about the rent, and the figure kept coming up. So I could never forget how much they paid. It was thirty-six bucks.

I couldn't bring myself to spend a month's rent on an hour's flight to Minnesota. I had too much of my mother in me. I said to Ritchie, "You go."

He shouldn't have said yes. Ritchie had a dread terror of airplanes. When he was a little kid, a plane crashed into his school playground, killing some of his schoolmates. His manager got him over the fear by showing how it would limit his career. Ritchie took the lesson all too well. He accepted my offer and took my seat.

Only the four of us knew who was getting on the plane when we left the dressing room that night. Of the four who were in that room, I'm the only one who survived beyond February 3, 1959.

The plane took off around one in the morning from the Mason City Municipal Airport. As it flew away, the plane's owner, watching from the tower, noticed the taillight begin to descend and then disappear. Air-traffic controllers tried to make contact by radio but got nothing. After daylight they found the wreckage in a cornfield, about five miles from the airport. The pilot and all three of my friends were dead.

* * *

There are times when clichés sound hollow. There are times when they sound cruel. The promoters, of course, were distraught by the news. They had a fondness for the guys, and they had a lot invested in the future of Buddy Holly, Ritchie Valens, and the Big Bopper. But they had no doubt about what they would tell us.

"The show must go on."

We met our obligations, every one of them, joined by Jimmy Clanton ("Just a Dream") and Bobby Vee, a sixteen-year-old from North Dakota who'd been profoundly influenced by Buddy Holly. The world would hear more from him in the years

44

ahead—"Take Good Care of My Baby" would hit number one—but this winter party was his big break.

We got back on our bus, but we weren't in the mood for singing. We felt a lot of survivor's guilt, and we discussed the events of February 2 over and over again. I told the story of the coin toss, and it went abroad from there, in various forms, picking up new characters and dramatic twists along the way.

It was a long, numb two weeks till the tour closed on February 18. I went back to New York and tried to go home. Every culture and every ethnic group has its own way of dealing with grief. In my family we bottled it up. We didn't say anything. And there weren't any grief counselors in the Bronx in 1959.

My knucklehead friends must have felt bad for me but didn't really know what to say. They'd try to get me interested in gang life again, to make me feel better. They'd invite me to go out and bust some heads. They didn't get it.

But frankly, neither did I. How do you make sense of something like this? I leaned on Susan, and I leaned into my addictions.

As much as I kept quiet, the story kept coming back to me, and in the most absurd forms. Some people used it to get the fifteen minutes of fame that Andy Warhol would one day promise everybody—but they were extending their time with a lot of Hamburger Helper.

If all the people who said they'd flipped a coin with Buddy Holly were telling the truth, we would've needed a military personnel carrier to fit them all. I didn't think the coin flip was important, because it was not the deciding factor for my taking the bus. But I guess a story like that makes for good TV, and it makes the guys respect you at the bar.

I found the whole business distasteful and even made an oblique reference to it in a song in the sixties. But Don McLean got more notice with his song about "the day the music died."

I prefer to think about it as the day the music was born. In Buddy Holly and the Crickets, rock music had found its lasting form: two guitars, a bass, and drums. The news of Buddy and his "widowed bride" touched a lot of people deep inside, and it made them love their music all the more, because they knew the artists were mortal. The songs may last forever, but we singers were trying to outrun the clock.

Years later I read a line about a natural process, and it seemed to provide a good analogy for what happened to us and to rock and roll back in 1959. Jesus told his disciples: "Truly, truly, I say to you, unless a grain of wheat falls into the earth and dies, it remains alone; but if it dies, it bears much fruit" (John 12:24).

7 TEENAGER IN TROUBLE

IN THE MONTHS THAT FOLLOWED the Winter Dance Party, my life took on a surreal quality. I was grieving. My heart was dragging in the depths, and I didn't know how to express it. I was angry, and I was stoned a lot of the time.

As if to make the experience more bizarre, in March—just a few weeks after the tour had ended—our next single, "A Teenager in Love," was released, and it shot up the national charts, reaching number five. We had cracked that elite club, the Top Ten, and had even made it into its upper half. We were much in demand—on television, on tour, on radio. No one could escape Dion and the Belmonts. My great problem was that I couldn't escape Dion.

"Teenager in Love" is a work of genius, one of the greatest songs crafted by one of the greatest songwriting teams in history, Doc Pomus and Mort Shuman. They wrote dozens of hits in rock's early years, the signature songs of the era, and they show up often in movies—songs like "Save the Last Dance for Me" and "This Magic Moment." "Teenager" was one of the first

Pomus-Shuman songs to soar so high. I may be prejudiced, but I think it's also their best.

When I was putting my arrangement together, the melody and harmonies seemed like a warm blanket of sound under me while I was floating freely on top. "Teenager" was like nothing I'd heard before; yet it also felt like something that had been floating in the air since the caveman. And it speaks to an experience that's fairly standard with human nature (at least in a certain phase of life).

By the end of the year 1959, the song held not just one but three positions in the British Top Twenty. After Dion and the Belmonts scored with it, British groups rushed in with their own covers.

> Each time we have a quarrel,
> it almost breaks my heart,
> because I'm so afraid that we will have to part.
> Each night I ask the stars up above:
> Why must I be a teenager in love?

There are two ways to take the song. You can take it straight, as a cry from the heart of a tortured adolescent, struggling with new and unfamiliar feelings; and many teens did take it that way. It spoke to their condition. They bought the record. They danced to it. They chose it repeatedly on the jukebox at the diner.

But there's another way to take the song. You can take it as a lighthearted portrayal of teen awkwardness—the bipolar condition that turns on a dime from self-pity to elation. You were a teenager once. You remember?

One day I feel so happy
Next day I feel so sad
I guess I'll learn to take the good with the bad
Each night I ask the stars up above:
Why must I be a teenager in love?[1]

Well, the guys who sang that song weren't too far removed from their teen years. We were able to sing the song in earnest for our teenaged audience, but it's self-deprecating enough to pass as irony with the grown-ups. As I said, it's sheer genius.

❊ ❊ ❊

"Teenager" was a work of genius. Me, I was just a piece of work. I was nineteen years old, and I still had that teen bipolar thing going, only chemically enhanced, so that the lows were lower and the highs were higher. And I was emotionally and spiritually equipped for none of this. I made the protagonist of that song look as even-keeled as Cary Grant.

Nineteen fifty-nine went, for me, like the stock market goes just before a crash. It kept going up, up, up. Our next release turned out to be my biggest hit with the Belmonts. "Where or When," our cover of a Rodgers and Hart show tune from the 1930s, debuted in November of that year and reached number three. That single really reflected the kind of smooth pop music that Carlo, Angelo, and Freddie wanted to do—and the kind of music the record company wanted us to do. In "Where or When," we did it well.

But it wasn't my kind of music. I wanted to rock out. I felt as if the Belmonts and I were growing apart. Some of it I could chalk up to artistic differences. We had different approaches to the music, different approaches to work. But some of it I chalk up to the wedge that drug addiction drives into any relationship. An addict isn't thinking primarily about you when he's talking to you. If he's not enjoying his most recent fix, he's planning for his next one. You're a point somewhere along that timeline —maybe a significant point but not the two that really matter. If I suffered estrangement from friends during those years, I take the blame.

But it was time to go it alone. With the support of the execs at the record company—whose name was now Laurie Records—I'd made the difficult decision to break from the Belmonts and go solo. I'm glad that the Belmonts and I were able to end on a high note, with our biggest hit.

* * *

In my private life though, I had no intention of going solo. I was still hanging with Susan, as we'd been doing since I was fifteen and she was thirteen. We couldn't imagine life without one another.

I don't want to give the wrong impression. Sometimes when I talk about Susan, I get so sappy I make her out to be a cross between Betsy Ross, Tammy Wynette, and the Statue of Liberty, a virtuous but enabling woman who perpetually carried a torch for a good-for-nothing man. That's not who she is.

I fell in love with Susan Butterfield because of her intelligence and wit and beauty but most of all because of her inner strength. I often say that she's a black belt in love, and I mean to evoke everything that goes with that metaphor: self-control, discipline, serenity. Her force may not be lethal, but it's precise. As sweet as she is, this "black belt in love" knows how to take my legs out from under me and the breath from out of my lungs.

At thirteen with my guitar, I was aspiring to be
Hank Williams. (Photo by Pat DiMucci.)

I formed the great Bronx group, Dion and the Belmonts. Here we are in my parents' little apartment. Left to right: Carlo Mastrangelo, Freddie Milano, yours truly, and Angelo D'Aleo. (Photo by Pat DiMucci.)

The soul of my Belmont neighborhood: Monsignor Pernicone and Mount Carmel Church.
(Photos courtesy of Our Lady of Mount Carmel parish, Bronx, N.Y.)

My lady Susan is radiant. I have to wear shades when I'm with her. Of course, she has to hold on to her hat when she's with me. (Easter 1958; photo by Pat DiMucci.)

A promo poster for the fateful Winter Dance Party tour. I'm the only headliner who lived to tell the story.

I wanted to impress Susan with all the "finer things" —room service, jewelry, flowers. She deserved it. She still does. (Photo courtesy of Dion Productions.)

My mom rocks on. Look at her: almost a hundred, and she still cooks a mean pasta. (Photo by Tom LaPointe.)

My dad still looked good in his nineties. (Photo by Dion DiMucci.)

A teenager's dream come true: my dinner with Gina Lollobrigida. (Photo by Ric Newman.)

My own painting of my guitar hero, the blues poet Robert Johnson. (Photo courtesy of Dion Productions.)

In a New York club with Lou Reed, who sang backups on *King of the New York Streets*. (Photo by Susan DiMucci.)

On stage with Jamie King Colton on sax. (Photo by Cathy LaMarca MacDonald.)

Me and the Boss, Bruce Springsteen.

I did Rome with Scott Hahn in 2000 and 2005. Here we are in St. Peter's Square. On this Rock… we rocked.
(Photo courtesy of Dion Productions.)

Me and my girls. Left to right: Tane, August, Lark. (Photo courtesy of Dion Productions.)

Susan and me: I'm no longer a teenager, but I'm still in love with the same girl I fell for when I was a kid on the streets. (Photo courtesy of Dion Productions.)

Yo! Some things never change. I've always got my guitar. (Photos courtesy of Dion Productions.)

Susan had grown up watching addiction up close. Her father struggled with the bottle, and he gradually prevailed over it. By the time she met me, Susan had already learned that the best way to love such a guy was not to indulge him but to be forthright and firm. Her delivery made it relatively painless. She was deadpan, and she was funny; but she was always on target.

She didn't know how bad off I was. I was careful not to let her know. Machismo mattered in my neighborhood. And the heroin was such a matter of shame to me that I hid it even from her. I didn't want her, or anyone else, to see my weakness.

Still, she wasn't blind, and she knew I wasn't a promising candidate for domestic bliss.

We had fun together, but I can't say our friendship was deepening. I was proud to hit the nightclubs with such a beautiful woman on my arm. But frankly, I didn't know what to do with all that. I didn't know how to *be* with a woman, how to love her, how to be her friend. I had no real models for this. Somewhere in my brain Monsignor's voice was echoing: "Then love her." But what did love mean anyway?

I had the vague intention to stay with her. She loved me, and she believed she could work with that—and with all the other stuff that came with me.

Poets compare their loves to red roses and summer days. I've written songs about Susan but never managed one that captures the wonder of it all. Her love is like God's love, a mystery I'll never fathom and never deserve.

8 JUST DION

DION—THE NAME STANDS OUT. It always has.

When my parents took me to be baptized, the priest insisted that they come up with another name, because he didn't recognize Dion as a saint's name. In fact, he didn't recognize Dion at all, and my father had no idea where he had picked up the name. So I was baptized Dion Francis.

Now, my friends in the theology business tell me the pastor was ill-informed. They rattle off a half-dozen old-time saints named "Dionysius" from places as exotic as Alexandria in Egypt and Athens in Greece. But in our Italian parish, we didn't cast the net so wide. Maybe Father was looking for an *Italian* saint, and so he got one in Francis.

I love Francis of Assisi. But Frankies were a dime a dozen in Belmont.

I could always answer confidently, though, to "Yo, Dion!" Even if I was standing in a crowd, I knew I was the only Dion in earshot.

53

Down the years the name has come in handy. It's memorable because it's different. That helps in show business. A first name like Dion is especially useful when you have an Italian surname that most Americans aren't sure how to pronounce. "Is it *Di-Mew-chee* or *Di-Moo-chee*?" In 1960 the folks in Fort Wayne, Indiana, were still getting used to the pronunciation of *pizza* and *lasagna*. *DiMucci* was just too much to add to their plate.

So when I decided to go solo, my record company made the wise decision to present me to my fans on a first-name basis.

It worked. The name was unusual enough, like Elvis, so nobody in his right mind was going to ask, "Which Dion do you mean?" Kids who had been buying records by Dion and the Belmonts had no trouble whatsoever switching to just Dion. The hits proved it.

"Lonely Teenager," from my album *Alone with Dion*, hit number twelve. We were building on the "Teenager" franchise, which had proven successful in "Teenager in Love." But this teenager was different. He was on his own, very much alone— hiding out, staying out of sight—but longing for a home.[1]

* * *

I had been playing around with another tune since I was a kid in the schoolyard. It stayed with me, and I kept coming back to it. I would play it on guitar while my buddies sang along with it and banged on boxes and cans. Then, with our voices, we'd imitate the sounds of saxes and horns like we heard at the Apollo Theater. We'd get a riff going, and we could keep it going for forty-five minutes, jamming with just our voices. I could never shake that basic riff, but I never managed to finish it up as a song.

But now I knew it was just the sound I wanted to rock the fans at the Brooklyn Fox.

I recruited one of the guys from the neighborhood, Ernie Maresca, to help me finish it up. I wanted this song to sound as fresh on vinyl as it did on the street. I wanted to keep it primitive—driven by hand claps, vocals, and a slight touch of drums. I wanted it to rock.

By the time we were done, it was "Runaround Sue." I knew we had something great.

> Here's my story, sad but true.
> It's about a girl that I once knew.
> She took my love, then ran around
> with every single guy in town.
> I should have known it from the very start.
> This girl would leave me with a broken heart.
> Now listen, people, what I'm telling you.
> Keep away from Runaround Sue.[2]

Ernie and I wrote it about a real girl in the neighborhood, but we changed the name to protect the guilty. She was the kind of girl who loved to be worshipped and worked hard to get a guy's attention; but as soon as she had him, she'd lose interest and start charming somebody else.

We used the name Sue because it fit and because it lends itself to a lot of rhymes—key to pop success.

Now, people, let me put you wise: Contrary to what has been reported everywhere, the song is *not* about the woman I married. It is not now, nor has it ever been, about Susan Butterfield DiMucci.

My poor wife has had to endure being introduced as "Runaround Sue" at least a thousand times since 1961. She smiles through it all. And she may one day be canonized for it. Even *The New York Times* (December 3, 2000) reported that she was the "inspiration" for the song. *The New York Times*!

Well, it's not the worst I've put her through. And the song has treated us pretty well. It hit number one in September 1961. A song doesn't score any higher than that.

❋ ❋ ❋

And the hits kept coming.

Later in 1961 I put together another one with Ernie Maresca, "The Wanderer." It became a signature for me.

> Well, I'm the type of guy who will never settle down.
> Where pretty girls are, well, you know that I'm around.
> I kiss 'em and I love 'em 'cause to me they're all the
>   same.
> I hug 'em and I squeeze 'em, they don't even know my
>   name.
> They call me the Wanderer,
> yeah, the Wanderer.
> I roam around, around, around.
> Well, there's Flo on my left, and there's Mary on my
>   right.
> And Janie is the girl that I'll be with tonight.
> And when she asks me which one I love the best,
> I tear open my shirt, and I got "Rosie" on my chest.

Lots of people observed that "The Wanderer" was maybe a male version of "Runaround Sue." And just as people assumed that "Sue" was about Susan, they assumed that "The Wanderer" was about me. In fact, I've had feminists rip me up for promoting a double-standard: "Sue" is someone to keep away from, but "The Wanderer" is "happy."

But that's not what the song says, and it's certainly not what I meant. Listen to the words:

> I roam from town to town
> and go through life without a care.
> I'm as happy as a clown
> with my two fists of iron, but I'm going nowhere.[3]

The Wanderer isn't happy. He's "as happy as a clown." And clowns are notoriously *un*happy characters. Growing up in an Italian neighborhood meant I grew up with opera. Have you ever listened to Leoncavallo's *Pagliacci*? Here's a rough translation of the most famous lines from "Ridi, Pagliaccio": "Laugh, clown, laugh at your broken love, laugh at the pain that poisons your heart!" If you don't have time for opera, just listen to Smokey Robinson's "Tears of a Clown," where the title character wears a smile "to fool the public." The clown's smile is painted on for a reason.

Bruce Springsteen is one of the few listeners who got "The Wanderer." He wrote me, "The line 'I got two fists of iron but I'm going nowhere' turns all of 'The Wanderer's' macho posturing back in on itself and grounds the music in real life."

(I like to think I can hear echoes of "The Wanderer" in the Boss's own songs. Each sentence in my hit starts on a downbeat, which Bruce does a lot these days. And then there's the sax solo. From Buddy Lucas to Clarence Clemons, what's rock and roll without a great sax solo?)

"The Wanderer" is a dark song, and I recorded it at a time when you weren't supposed to get so dark with pop music. It genuinely surprised me when it shot to number two.

But maybe it shouldn't have. This was the kind of rock I wanted to play. It was the sound my friends and I had in our heads when we were coming home, late at night, from the Apollo in Harlem. In fact, I was now recording with so many of the guys we used to pay to see at the Apollo: Panama Francis on drums, Sticks Evans on percussion, Big Buddy Lucas on tenor saxophone, and Jerome Richardson on alto sax. It was a dream come true for me to be playing with my heroes. I couldn't wait to strap on my guitar and rock out with those guys.

* * *

Laurie Records didn't share my enthusiasm, however. They thought it was just a matter of time before my fans outgrew rock and roll. So they wanted me to move a step ahead and start recording standards, chestnuts, and evergreens from the Golden Age of Tin Pan Alley—the stuff you heard on the radio when you went to the dentist. To me a root canal seemed more pleasant.

I had an aggressive manager, Sal Bonefetti, who understood that the music was important to me. He also helped me understand that the record company wasn't paying me all the royalties that belonged to me.

Sal had a crazy plan. He thought he could use my market appeal—demonstrated by now through several platinum records—to sell me to Columbia Records. Now, Columbia was the biggest in the business, but they didn't stoop to dirty their hands with rock and roll. They catered to "mature" and "adult" tastes. I thought Sal's ultimate goal was overly ambitious.

But you know what? He was right. He got me signed for five years, at a hundred thousand dollars a year—guaranteed. Even if I never scored a hit, I would still pull down the big paycheck. I was the first rock artist to be signed to Columbia.

And I did score the hits: "Ruby Baby," "Drip Drop," and "Donna the Prima Donna" (a tongue-in-cheek tribute to my sister) all went to the top of the charts. Columbia had made an auspicious debut in the world of rock music; and I was recording the songs I was born to sing and play.

Columbia wanted to expand their business and improve distribution in Europe, Canada, and South America. So Sal booked me for tours, starting with South America—Rio de Janeiro, Buenos Aires, Caracas, Uruguay. For Columbia, for Sal, and for my career, it was a tremendous success. The audiences were wonderful. The people did their best to make me comfortable.

But I was miserable and alone. Wherever we went, I couldn't speak the language, and there was no one I really wanted to talk to anyway. I've never been much of a shopper or spender, so I didn't want to go anywhere. I spent a lot of time in hotel rooms, alone, thinking of how much I missed Susan. I'd become a devilish parody of my musical persona: *alone with Dion...lonely teenager...happy as a clown...going nowhere....*

I had made it out of the neighborhood. I had made it on my own, apart from the Belmonts. I had made it to the top of my profession. I had made so much money that I didn't ever need to worry about the things that consumed my mom and dad. I had made it. Nobody in my family had won like this. I had everything I ever wished for, and I was miserable and alone, far from "home where I belong."

And where could I find such a home anyway? In a hotel room in Montevideo, Uruguay, I put the question; and for the first time, I glimpsed an answer.

8 JUST DION

9 FROM TOP TO BOTTOM

10 I KNOW JACK

SUSAN BUTTERFIELD AND I MARRIED on March 25, 1963. We had the ceremony in a Unitarian church in New York. We wanted a church wedding, like everybody does, though we didn't go to church. My manager suggested the Unitarians because they were known to tolerate everyone and everything, and they wouldn't ask too many questions or require anything from us.

But the religious part of the day meant little to me. I was looking for a reason to hope, and a future with Susan was the only horizon that held out any promise to me. To be home, to be at peace—it's what we all want, whether we're the "Lonely Teenager" or the rising teen idol. Susan and I made our dream home on the Hudson River, and that won me something more than a pile of hit records ever could. I wish I could say that I understood that at the time, but I didn't have a clue.

Nor did I notice that our wedding day was the Feast of the Annunciation, the day the Church celebrates the angel's tidings to the Virgin Mary, just a little girl in a village in the middle of nowhere. She would soon become the Mother of God

Almighty, and with her Son she would change the world. So whether I knew it or not, it was a great day for new beginnings.

¤ ¤ ¤

My years with Columbia were big years. It was a world very different from Mohawk/Laurie. Columbia was a big business, with big money, big offices, and big ideas buzzing around the long hallways. The young lawyer who signed my checks was Clive Davis, who would soon soar to president of the company and then go on to be founder and president of his own record label, Arista.

But for me the real power center was the office of John Hammond. John was Columbia's premier talent scout, famous for his role in the career of so many musical revolutionaries—from Benny Goodman, Billie Holiday, and Count Basie to Pete Seeger, Aretha Franklin, and yours truly. John had been around forever, and by the time I got to Columbia, he was already a legend in the music business. But he wore it lightly. His office door was always open, and you could hear the most amazing sounds coming from inside. Sometimes it was a scratchy old 78-rpm record from the 1920s. Sometimes it was his latest find, somebody like Aretha Franklin, belting out a hymn.

I often say that John was a head with a heart, while his son, the famous bluesman, also named John Hammond, is a heart with a head. The elder Hammond loved music with all of that gigantic heart, and you could see it in his expression when you peeked into his office. He loved music the way a good man loves his wife, and he could sit there and just bask in it, with an expression of pure joy.

But then, if he waved you into the office, you got the full ben-
efit of the Hammond brain, a trove of musicology, culture, history, and wild personal experience. He could lean back in his
chair while the music played away and trace for you the lines of
tradition and influence that ran from a street corner in New
Orleans in the 1890s to a garage band in suburban New Jersey
in the 1960s.

John was a native New Yorker, like me, but we grew up in different circumstances. He was a blueblood, descended from the
Vanderbilts, Ivy-League educated in law, and classically trained
in music. I was full-blooded Bronx, and I picked up my music,
like everything else, on the streets where I lived. But those were
some of the same streets John was prowling to hear sounds that
were fresh and raw. He also trolled the Baptist churches and
back-alley bars of the Deep South, always with his ear keen for
the local music. He loved the Delta blues best of all, and that's
the stuff he laid on me one day when I followed the trail of
sound that led to his desk.

His greeting was almost always the same: "Dion, listen to
this."

"This" was his personal copy of an album John had just
released: "King of the Delta Blues Singers," by Robert Johnson,
a man who had died almost a quarter-century earlier.

"Dion, this album sold twenty-five thousand records entirely
by word of mouth."

I was unimpressed. Hey, I'd cut several million-selling
records in the past few months alone.

But then John dropped the needle into the grooves, and I
heard the voice of a man, very much alive—more alive than I
was—singing blues with just his guitar for accompaniment.

I can compare that moment to only one other in my life: that Sunday when I was eleven years old and I heard Hank Williams for the first time. Johnson's raw Delta blues worked on me the same way. If I were a more demonstrative kind of Italian, I would have dropped to my knees or wept. His blues were speaking to something inside me—and tearing it out of me, violently. The blues were like no drug I had known. I knew I needed more.

* * *

Success is a funny thing. You can gain it and think you own it, but really it owns you. That's why recording artists are such an insecure breed. Holding on to fame comes to take priority over doing what we love. Anything we accomplish is fleeting. The fans are fickle. The American attention span is notoriously short.

If the situation makes artists insecure, it's worse for the record-company executives. They get positively paranoid, and they try to move singers like chess pieces, anticipating the next trend and repositioning the artists to prepare for it. I can't blame them. They invest a lot of money in building up somebody's name. They want to see a long-term return on that investment.

Through the first half of the 1960s, the record labels were still expecting the sun to set on rock and roll. Even though Columbia signed me to get a piece of the action, they didn't really think it could last. They wanted to groom me to be the next Sinatra. But with "The Wanderer" and "Runaround Sue," I was just beginning to find my own voice as a rocker and as a writer. Here's the way the music-historian Greg Shaw described what I was doing, in the pages of *Rolling Stone* magazine:

Dion was the original punk. Stand him up next to his contemporary male teen idols—Frankie Avalon, Fabian, Bobby Vee...Paul Anka, Neil Sedaka...and the difference is obvious. They were all simpering, heartstruck, crybabies, with the possible exception of Fabian, and the best he could come up with was *"yay yay yay I'm like a tiger"* which, needless to say, was somewhat less than convincing. But when Dion sang *"I love 'em and I leave 'em, they don't even know my name!"* there was no doubting him. He was tough, arrogant, not really dangerous like Elvis, but unquestionably mean. A punk.

And in 1960–62, he was the best thing we had. Not only did he have the image, he also had a succession of great songs perfectly suited to his style, written by himself and Ernie Maresca; and to top it off he had the very best voice around, kinda rough but capable of all kinds of intonations, and a sure, instinctive sense of style and delivery that elevated his records to a plane far above the ordinary. He never had to reach or strain for a note, never sounded forced or contrived. His records were smooth, natural, honest, earthy, and vastly appealing.[1]

When a man is doing what he loves and doing it well, he knows it. In my first years at Columbia, I knew it.

✺ ✺ ✺

John Hammond may have been Columbia's main man in artist relations, but by immersing me in the Delta blues, he drew me still further away from the place where Columbia wanted me to be. The blues became an obsession. I couldn't get enough of the records, and John was always eager to recommend more. I did what I could to bring the big names to New York, so I could hear them play. I traveled to the festivals for the same reason. I had the privilege to spend time with some of my new heroes, men like Skip James and the Reverend Gary Davis, when they were at their peak.

So there was Columbia Records trying to stuff me into a tuxedo so I could sing the Cole Porter songbook. Meanwhile I was going Delta on them.

You've probably heard the Willie Dixon song "Spoonful." I first heard it sung by Howlin' Wolf in 1960. It would become a hit for Eric Clapton and Cream in 1966. A couple years before Cream charted with it, I tried to take it into the mainstream, recording my own rendition with a group of great musicians from the Apollo Theatre.

"Spoonful" is a two-chord groove, a love song of sorts but with a dark and sinister side. In the lyrics a man compares a "spoonful" of his lady's love to a spoonful of diamonds or gold, coffee or tea, and so on. The lady's love, of course, is greater than all these things. The song ends, however, with a veiled threat if the woman should ever be unfaithful. The final "spoonful"? Lead from his forty-five-caliber pistol.

Columbia didn't quite warm to it, but they humored me. And I certainly wasn't the last "alternative" act they signed. Soon after me came Bob Dylan, who was new to the label but not new to me. I had actually met him on the fateful Winter Dance Party Tour. Back then he went by the stage name Elston Gunnn. He played keyboards for Buddy Holly's replacement, Bobby Vee. Dylan was another regular in John Hammond's office and another devotee of Robert Johnson. We shared the same producer at Columbia, Tom Wilson.

* * *

As I said, those were big years. And wherever I went, I got treated in a big way. I was supposed to be the advance guard of Columbia's big breakthrough in Europe. They booked a tour for me that was even more lavish than my South American circuit.

This time, though, I knew better. I insisted on taking Susan with me, and as we booked the gigs I ensured that everywhere we went she and I would have the best of everything: penthouse suites, choice wines, banquets, fresh flowers, all by room service. Every time we stepped out of a hotel, she was on my arm, looking gorgeous, and the flashbulbs were popping. People were singing my songs in the streets.

It couldn't have gone any better. All I wanted was to look into her eyes and see her hero reflected there. I saw love looking back at me.

One night in France we were sitting at one of our candlelight dinners, and she was unusually quiet. Then she said to me, "Dion, is this all you want? I mean, is this it?"

I didn't know what she was getting at. Hadn't I ordered enough flowers? Was something wrong with the wine?

No, I knew she was asking me something profound, but I didn't know what it was. I couldn't know what it was.

What *did* I want? How could I want for anything? I had the job, the girl, the good stuff. Didn't I have everything anybody could want?

If I did, why did I still feel miserable inside?

Susan scared me with her questions. I couldn't answer them. And they wouldn't go away.

٭ ٭ ٭

Today, as I write this, after so many decades clean and sober, all my years of using and boozing seem to collapse into a single point.

There's a certain sameness to memoirs of drug use. It's a tired story of need and desperation, misbehavior and criminal activity. Yada, yada, yada. The cycle plays itself out and plays itself over.

Once upon a time such stories were shocking. But in my opinion, they got tiresome many years ago, and I will not subject you to yet another drugalog. You want to know something? Addicts do outrageous things—no kidding, big news—and they still manage to be crashing bores.

I used heroin for fourteen years. Many (maybe most) addicts don't drag it out that long. They give it up, or they die. But those years are now just a small portion of my life. I moved on more than forty-two years ago. I've already talked enough about those years in other places. (Google it if you really want to know.) So I won't subject you to the cold sweats and the questionable syringes in darkened stairwells.

It ended for me in a way that's fairly typical—by stages—but each stage began with an event that was extraordinary and maybe even miraculous.

٭ ٭ ٭

I had tried to go the medical route, twice. Once the executives at the record company checked me into a celebrity retreat in Connecticut. It didn't work. Then, years later, I tried to check myself into a couple hospitals. I was in such bad shape that even the hospitals wouldn't take me.

I didn't have the will to do it. But I knew I couldn't keep going the way I was going. I had married Susan because I loved her, and I believed that her love was the only thing that could save me. I believed I could get responsible for her sake—though so far I hadn't made good on that intention. The thought of losing her terrified me, but terror couldn't get me sober. Fear just made me want to get stoned.

So the fears just got worse—irrational and paranoid. Once I "saw" a heroin dealer morph into the devil, right before my eyes. I knew it was a hallucination, but he didn't seem out of place. I was living in hell.

When Susan told me she was pregnant with our first child, I knew I'd have to go straight. That's when I found a hospital that would take me in, and I somehow managed to shake loose of the heroin. Even with such high motivation though, I couldn't give up the rest. I was still drinking, and for the shows I was popping pills for confidence. The occasions were fewer though.

By 1964 Columbia and I were coming to a parting of the ways. I had no clear sense of direction, and I found it hard to sustain interest in the music. I'd always been frugal with my money, but it was going down the tubes faster and faster, on drugs and alcohol. This was the bleakest, darkest period of my life. I was irritable, restless, discontented. I had a soul sickness that was killing me slowly. I did a lot of things that were selfish, dishonest, inconsiderate, fearful, and cruel.

In 1968 Susan and I weren't doing well—that's an understatement—so we figured we'd try to start again. We did what New Yorkers do in such circumstances. We moved to Florida, where her family was living.

⑩ I KNOW JACK

I WAS ABOUT TO BECOME a father, but in many ways I was still an adolescent punk. I acted as if Susan was still my girlfriend, and I had no real desire to get to know her family.

Her dad, Jack Butterfield, wasn't the kind of guy I hung out with anyway. He smiled too much. He read from a prayer book every morning before he had his breakfast. Everything about him annoyed me, yet nothing ever seemed to disturb his peace. Bad traffic, bad weather—he took it all in stride.

I didn't want to know anybody like that. But I guess I had no choice, since we were living in his house while we looked for our own place.

The thing that irritated me most about him was his cheerfulness. Jack was a giant of a man, but with gentle, pale blue eyes that started smiling the moment he got out of bed.

We'd be sitting at the breakfast table early in the morning, and maybe I was feeling a little hung over, and he'd say to me, "Dee, would you listen to that?"

"What?"

"Listen to those birds. Aren't they amazing?"

His manner ran like fingernails across the blackboard in my brain.

Why? I'll tell you why. If that guy was right, I had to be mistaken. His happiness was a damning reproach to my misery. If he could find a way to get through life in peace—in spite of some pretty big challenges—then that meant I was a failure.

Not in a million years could I admit the possibility that I might be wrong. Nor could I accept a judgment that I was a failure. Just look at my gold records! By then there were eleven of them hanging on the wall. When was the last time Jack Butterfield played a sold-out show in a major venue? When was the last time he appeared on network TV or in *Time* magazine? Just who did he think he was?

Yet there I was, looking at a guy who had something I wanted—something I couldn't even imagine ever having: real serenity. He was relaxed, confident, peaceful, and strong.

Me, I felt lousy about life. I was angry. And I could list off all the people who were to blame for my misery: my mother, my father, the Church, the neighborhood, the record industry. My wife! Susan was always nearby, and so she was easy to blame.

How was I gonna hear the freaking birds over all the anger, frustration, resentment, anxiety, and fear that were making noise in my head?

As much as he annoyed me, I felt drawn to Jack. I wanted to see him in action. I wanted to see him at work—he was maître at a classy club, with fifty people working for him. I wanted to see him with friends, at the hardware store, mowing the lawn.

Watching him was, for me, like watching a *National Geographic* documentary about the behavior of a remote tribe on some island I'd never heard of. A tribe of normal people. Happy people. Kind people. Trusting people.

One night I got home from doing what I was always doing, and I tried to move quietly down the hallway. As I passed Jack's bedroom, I saw that giant down on his knees by his bed, as if he was a little kid. I almost cried.

Maybe a couple nights later I mentioned to him in passing that I'd like him to pray for me. "Oh, Dion," he said, "you should try praying yourself. God loves to hear from strangers."

It wasn't the last time he found a subtle way of making the suggestion. He liked to quote the Scripture, "Ask, and it will be given you" (Matthew 7:7).

So one night I tried it. I got down on my knees, just as I'd seen Jack doing, and in my inimitable, rambling way, I asked God to take away my obsession with alcohol, to break the chains.

And he did—just like that. Since that moment I've never taken a drink or done drugs. I've never wanted to. It was as if God was just waiting for me to ask.

Now, I'm nothing like the apostle John. I don't have end-times visions. But I can imagine one Last Judgment scenario very vividly.

There, before the throne of God, is a huge multitude of people, and they're all shaking their fists at him and complaining about this situation and that situation, and each person ends his complaint with "Why didn't you do something?"

And then God says to all of us, "Why didn't you ask?"

Up till that moment on April 1, 1968, I had been too proud to ask. I already knew all the answers. I already had everything under control. I had to *lose* control. I had to fail, utterly and undeniably. I had to see that I was powerless and surrender. I had to acknowledge my weakness and ask the Almighty for help—to let him be all mighty on my turf. "When I am weak, then I am strong" (2 Corinthians 12:10).

It was Jack the strong, Jack the giant, who showed me how to be little and weak, God's child, just as he was.

◦ ◦ ◦

As I got to know Jack, I learned more about his past. He too had been addicted to drink, though by 1968 he'd been sober for fourteen years—almost exactly as long as I'd been drunk.

I got involved in a spiritually based twelve-step recovery program, and I began to meet other people who had struggled and were winning. For the first time in my life, I let myself learn from others. One man in particular became a mentor to me, and he remains so to this day. I won't embarrass him by mentioning his name. He's a humble guy but very smart and very good with words. Early on he helped me see that sobriety was only the beginning of a cure. I still had many of the problems that were part of the disease.

Exhibit A: my temper.

I wanted to control everything, and I freaked when I felt things were getting out of control. If I sensed that Susan was disagreeing with me, I tried to regain control by yelling. I was a virtuoso at yelling. I had a fondness for a certain four-letter Saxon word. It seemed to articulate whatever frustration or anger I was feeling, especially if I yelled it loud enough—and most especially if I broke something, like a lamp, when I was yelling it. Acting that way, I knew I could regain control of a room. Everybody else shut up, didn't they?

Once I was telling my mentor-friend about how I'd broken a lamp, and he looked a little shocked. He said, "Dion, I want you to promise me something: Next time you find yourself in a disagreement, you won't get up from your chair."

So I made the promise. And next time I didn't get up. Instead I stayed seated and broke what was at hand. I think it was a glass.

Later on I told my friend, and he looked at me with this pained expression. I wasn't getting what he meant. "Dion, next time you disagree with your wife, I want you to put your hands in your pockets."

I wanted to learn, so I did what he said. Next time Susan and I disagreed, I sat there with my hands in my pockets while I shouted every profanity I knew in her direction.

My buddy looked pained again. "Dion, listen to me," he said. "From now on, when you find yourself in a disagreement, why don't you just shut up and listen? You might be sitting across the table from someone who's frustrated."

He needed to get through a very thick skull. "From now on," he said, "unless *the Holy Spirit himself* tells you to speak, don't say *anything*. Just shut up."

I did, and I started to listen, and the woman I came to know was even more beautiful than the dazzling beauty I had married. I came to know Susan, for the first time, as not only my girl, not only the mother of our daughter, but as a friend.

I came around, eventually, to confront my other angers. With my parents and sisters I simply resigned. I called them together and told them I was giving up the overwhelming sense of responsibility I felt for fixing their problems. I was returning it to my father, to whom it properly belonged.

Then there was the Church. I told my buddy about why I was angry with the Church. I laid out my theories about how the Church was so manipulative and repressive. And he just sat back and listened. When I was done he said, "And when did you put these theories into place? Were you drinking at the time?"

Whoa, that was painful. I immediately saw my thoughts in the cold morning light.

"Let me suggest something," he said, "Why don't you put that issue—Church, God—on the shelf, and later you might want to revise your theory." He didn't push me or tell me what to think. He just helped me see that my life was in need of some second thoughts.

And some of those second thoughts were liberating. For the first time in my life, I was able to understand people who made me angry. I was able to forgive them. I was able to love them.

✻ ✻ ✻

When's a train most free, on the tracks or off?

When's a fish most free, in the water or out of it?

As a rocker I was all about freedom, but I had no idea what I was talking about. I thought freedom was having no constraints. But why be free if not for love's sake? And whoever heard of love that doesn't constrain the lovers?

Freedom isn't the ability to do whatever you want. It's the ability to choose the good. Until April 1, 1968, I had been unable to choose the good. I was doing whatever I felt like doing. But I was in bondage. What I wanted to do was drink. What I wanted to do was yell. What I wanted to do was not good for me or anybody else. The more I did it, the less free I was. "You will know the truth, and the truth will make you free" (John 8:32).

I was thinking about freedom a lot that year. I wasn't worried so much about music. I didn't really have a record deal at the moment, and I didn't really care. I was trying to learn how to live.

The news that year was all about freedom. It was the year after the so-called Summer of Love, when a hundred thousand young people converged on San Francisco for a countercultural orgy. Now there were riots in the cities and strikes on the college campuses.

Then, in April and June, came the assassinations of Martin Luther King, Jr., and Bobby Kennedy. It seemed, to a lot of people, that certain high ideals of our society had been buried with those men. We were roused to admiration for their sacrifice, but we were also wondering if America had the goods to live up to such standards.

At the time I was talking again with my old friends at Laurie Records, and they made me aware of a song that, for me, summed up the restless spirit of that year. It was called "Abraham, Martin, and John."

> Has anybody here, seen my old friend Abraham?
> Can you tell me where he's gone?
> He freed a lot of people, but it seems the good, they
>   die young.
> I just looked around and he's gone.[1]

The verses look at the lives of four American men who fought for social change and were assassinated for their efforts: Abraham Lincoln, John F. Kennedy, Martin Luther King, and Bobby Kennedy. The song wasn't a political statement. It certainly wasn't partisan. It is about two Democrats—JFK and

RFK—and two Republicans—MLK and Honest Abe. It is about basic human virtues and fundamental American principles. The message is simple: You can kill the dreamer, but you can't kill the dream. We will pick it up, and we'll carry it on.

I loved the song, and I put together a quiet, simple interpretation. It made it to the airwaves very quickly, while the events were still painfully recent, and all the qualities that had appealed to me proved to be universally appealing. It shot to the top of everybody's charts.

I was back to making music, but it was different now. I was different now. The records reflected it, even in their titles: *Sit Down, Old Friend*; *You're Not Alone*; *Sanctuary*.

I took to the praying business, too. I wasn't a churchgoer, but I recognized that anything good that was happening in my life wasn't happening through my own efforts. My prayers were regular, but they were kind of generic and impersonal—aimed upward at the Creator and master of my destiny. I experienced God's power long before I came to know him by name. On one of my first "sober albums," I included my interpretation of the song "He's Got the Whole World in His Hands."

My evangelical neighbors urged me to take another step and get to know Jesus Christ. So I started reading, and I fell in love with the Bible. I couldn't get enough of it. I would read St. Paul's letters to Timothy and weep uncontrollably because of their beauty.

I could identify with Paul, a big sinner, headstrong, who had undergone a rather sudden conversion. He showed me that I could put my faith in Jesus.

I wanted to be closer to Jesus. So I did what I had learned to do back in 1968. On December 14, 1979, I *asked* for it. I was out jogging, like every morning. As I went along I prayed, "God, it would be nice to be closer to you."

Suddenly I was flooded with white light. It was everywhere, inside me, outside me—everywhere. Ahead of me I saw a man with his arms outstretched. "I love you," he said. "Don't you know that? I'm your friend. I laid down my life for you. I'm here for you now."

That moment changed me every bit as much as the first time I dropped to my knees. Yet here's something mysterious: The more I changed, the more I became myself. God was, and still is, finishing up his creation.

11 HOPE IS HOMEMADE

FROM HARD EXPERIENCE SUSAN AND I knew that the world could be a dangerous place. We decided we were going to make our home a haven. Our children would know a kind of peace I never knew as a kid.

It's not that we abandoned the world and left it to spin itself out. We both felt a lot of gratitude toward the people who had helped me sober up. We decided we would become like them, and we've given much of our time as volunteers for twelve-step programs, counseling addicts and their families, visiting prisons and schools, and meeting with groups and individuals.

But we always put the children first. It didn't come naturally to me, because I didn't have good models for it. My childhood played out to a soundtrack of my parents' yelling. Left to my own instincts, I would have been a disaster of a dad. I'd learned, however, to listen to Susan and to watch her; and one of the things I found out was that she is a natural mother. More than that, she's one of nature's prodigies of motherhood.

I'm an amateur painter. It's one of the many things I picked up from my father. I paint what fascinates me, and I find that I return to two subjects: bluesmen (for obvious reasons) and mothers with children. I paint what's beautiful to me, what brings me joy.

My eldest daughter, Tane, was born near the end of 1966, and her early years coincided with my first years of clear thinking. It was as if I'd suddenly fallen upward and backward into Eden. Ours was a happy home because Tane was (as she remains to this day) so lovely, but also because I didn't have to be the center of our world anymore. It wasn't about me and my grievances anymore. It was about us.

We all grow up with the voices of our parents echoing inside us. They're either praising us or blaming us. My parents were never eager to accentuate the positive, so my inner voice was critical and loud. Mediterranean folks have even found ways to enshrine their negativity in superstitions. It's a peasant Italian folk belief—I'm not making this up—that if you praise your children, your praise will turn to a curse against their good qualities. I'm sure it all started as a check on vanity and pride; but believe me, it picked up some serious dysfunction along the way.

I never knew life could be different till, one day, Susan and I were driving somewhere with Tane in the backseat of the car. She must have been seven or eight. Out of nowhere she said to me, "Dad, I found out something. I found out I'm very intelligent."

My first thought could have come from my own parents. I thought to myself, *Well, you're pretty conceited*. And I almost opened my mouth, but something held me back.

And I heard Susan say something that made my jaw drop. She said, "How humble."

I whispered to Susan, "Humble?"

Susan said, "She's just recognizing God's gift."

So I asked Tane, "How do you know you're intelligent?"

She said, "I don't know. I just know it."

The great Catholic Scripture scholar Erasmus said that humility is truth, and that's something Susan instinctively knew. Humility is not self-loathing. It's seeing yourself as you are: a child of God who's maybe got some issues to work out, but a child of God nonetheless.

Tane, for her part, got the message of the psalm: "I am fearfully and wonderfully made!" (see Psalm 139:14).

And she is indeed.

* * *

Our second daughter, Lark, has lived up to her name. She's always been a singer like her dad and always a bit impetuous, in an artistic way (like her dad).

I remember once, when she was very small, she "ran away from home," and she actually made it quite a distance—still in town but far enough to scare Mom and Dad. She was nervous about her grades. So I held her close and explained, as well as I could, the difference between love and approval. Her mother and I would always love her, unconditionally—the way God loves her—and would never, ever withhold that love. That's how God is with all of us. We might not approve of everything Lark does, and we'd let her know about that. But we would still love her, "no matter whether you get A's or B's or C's."

She asked a logical but telling question: "What about D's and F's?"

Lark was (and is) as much a girl as I'm a boy. She developed into quite a singer, and when she was a teenager, I asked if she'd like to join me on tour.

She excitedly said yes. Then she added, "Oh, no! I'll need to shop for clothes!"

I said, "Honey, this is rock and roll. You go to Sears. You get a couple pairs of jeans. You're set."

She had other ideas. She went shopping. And when she went on tour with me, she looked like a princess—surrounded by a band of frogs in blue jeans, but a princess nonetheless.

✳ ✳ ✳

August, our youngest, loved to be in on secrets and surprises. I took her shopping with me on Valentine's Day, around 1977. She was maybe three years old.

We were on a secret mission to buy Mom a present. We snuck out to a shopping mall in Miami, but we failed as spies almost as soon as we got there. An NBC news crew was doing a sweet-on-the-street feature for the holiday, and they recognized me. Over they came, and I introduced them to August. The guy with the microphone said, "Oh, get the camera on her." So they did. And he said, "Now, pick up your daughter and have her kiss you."

So I picked her up and held her and said, "Go ahead. Kiss Daddy right here." I pointed to my cheek.

She hid behind my head.

So I asked her again. She burrowed deeper into my collar. We took three shots at it. She wasn't going to kiss me on camera. No way.

The guy with the microphone said, "Don't worry about it," and we went on our way and bought our gift for Mom. As soon as I got home, I took the present and hid it in our walk-in closet. And while I was leaning over, August walked into the closet and grabbed my neck and gave me a big kiss, saying, "I love you, Daddy." Nice.

Well, didn't I go to church that Sunday, and the Gospel I heard had Jesus saying, "But when you pray, go into your room and shut the door and pray to your Father who is in secret; and your Father who sees in secret will reward you" (Matthew 6:6)? And I saw, once again, that the Gospel is written all over the family when the family's living in the Gospel.

12 REIMAGINING JOHN

IT'S AMAZING WHAT CAN BRING back musical memories. As I was setting up to write one chapter, I got a call for an interview from *Rolling Stone* magazine, and the reporter got my thinking on a far different track.

He wanted me to come up with a fifteen-song playlist of music that's been influential to me. Talk about your killer homework assignment. Of course, my first draft was probably closer to a hundred songs. So I limited myself to the 1950s, and I decided to focus on guitar rock, since that's what I love and that's what I do.

I whittled it down. And I noticed something as I approached the final cut. I knew most of the guys on the list. I'd toured with some of them. But one thing I could say about each and every one of them, they were all tortured souls. They had something gnawing at their insides, and it came out in their music.

Take Gene Vincent, the guy who sang "Be-Bop-A-Lula" and died too young. He held on to a microphone as if it was his lifeline to somewhere. When he sang the sweat poured from him.

Gene had a bad leg, and he often had to be hospitalized after his shows because of the strain he put on his body. You might say he didn't have to do it that way. But he'd probably say he knew no other way to do it.

Hank Williams was on the list, of course, and Johnny Cash, Robert Johnson, Howlin' Wolf, Elvis Presley. Unless a guy has something eating at him, I'm not really interested in hearing his music.

* * *

John Lennon was that way. His upbringing made mine look like an episode of *Ozzie and Harriet*. Abandoned by his parents, he was raised by an aunt. With his mates in the Beatles, he achieved an early fame that was unprecedented and colossal—a fame made possible only by the electronic global village where we found ourselves in 1963. No amount of schooling or coaching could have prepared him for what came afterward.

Dick Clark talked to me about influence, but in the 1950s it was mostly a matter of groove, drive, and style. *How old are you? Where are you from? What kind of toothpaste do you use? Are you going steady?* In the 1960s rock stars were expected to hold forth on religion, politics, morals, you name it.

That pretty much started with Bob Dylan, who set a new and very high standard of thinking for rock and rollers. The Beatles followed suit, and John was the most outspoken of the four.

It's a pity he was treated like an oracle when he'd hardly started shaving. He wanted good things—we all do—but had no experience to speak of and little knowledge.

It didn't matter. The reporters needed copy, and they had deadlines. So they set him up to say things like his observation that the Beatles were more popular in America than Jesus. John said it, and I'm sure he regretted saying it, but he was describing what he thought was a pathetic situation. All the nuance was lost, however, in the six-word headlines.

I didn't care what he thought of war or the latest prime minister. I just loved his music. So I have happy memories of him. I remember walking the streets of Manhattan with him and Ringo Starr, window-shopping. We ducked into a store at Fifty-Seventh Street and Fifth Avenue, where we both gravitated to the same leather jacket. Luckily there were two. We both ended up wearing it on album covers. You can see his on *Rubber Soul*.

John loved my single "Ruby Baby." The Beatles used to cover it when they played in Hamburg, Germany, and at the Cavern Club in Liverpool. When they put together their masterpiece album, *Sgt. Peppers Lonely Hearts Club Band*, they worked up a collage of photographs and wax figures on the cover. They included only two American rock musicians, Bob Dylan and yours truly. I'm told that each of the Beatles picked the faces they wanted to include. I'm guessing John picked mine, because it's the image from the sleeve of "Ruby Baby," simply cut and pasted.

Maybe that was his way of acknowledging his influences, as I did in my playlist for *Rolling Stone*. I like to think so.

* * *

As I said earlier, if something's not eating you, I'm not interested in your music.

You'll notice something about the best rock and rollers: They tend to be outsiders. When they were kids they were loners.

They didn't fit in. They felt excluded. They made music to ease their pain. The great thing about writing a song is that it enables you to present a huge problem—loneliness, betrayal, fear, rejection—and then resolve it in three minutes and five seconds. All it takes is a few verses, a chorus, and a guitar solo.

The problem is that nothing's *really* resolved at the end of the song. The pain's still there, inside, even when the teenaged outsider becomes the consummate insider—and that's exactly what happens to the greatest rockers.

The pain remains; and if you don't find a way of dealing with it, you die. That's the way it ended for too long a litany of rockers. They died from overdose, self-abuse, or reckless living. Others died inside. Some went crazy, or just burned out, or turned into misanthropes.

But others grew up, which is, I think, the better way. At some point you need to grow up, even if you're a rock star.

If you grow up, maybe you realize that what you have in that microphone (or guitar or piano) is an international communications tool at your disposal. Harry Chapin grew up, and he used his celebrity to good ends. He worked it hard, too. If that guy cornered you at a party, he was going to win you over to his cause or wear you down. (I think the Lord called him home, in a freak auto accident, because Harry needed a rest!)

Bono is another example. His songs give him access to world leaders and the opinion pages of *The New York Times*. He uses every bit of it. Bruce Springsteen, too, has grown up and into his stardom.

Those who get some leverage from their celebrity have John Lennon to thank. He was the first to stage publicity stunts for his causes, demonstrating that he had the media at his beck and call. Put a camera on him, and he was going to talk about peace, not toothpaste.

I think his intentions were good, though he wasn't the most informed participant on the scene, and the drugs got in the way of his clear thinking. Nowhere is the murk of his thought more evident than in the most popular song of his solo years.

"Imagine" has become an anthem for internationalism—one-world government—and a favorite hymn for those who are "spiritual but not religious."

> Imagine there's no heaven —
> it's easy if you try —
> no hell below us,
> above us only sky.
> Imagine all the people
> living for today.[1]

John was a beautiful man, but this song represents a huge failure of imagination. In 1971 we didn't need to imagine atheistic internationalism. Communism was living and active, in at least two forms, and it wasn't producing peace. The Eastern Bloc was a repressive, unhappy place. China was sustaining its self-holocaust into Chairman Mao's senility. What made it possible for so many leaders to issue the orders for atrocities over the course of a half-century and more? They feared neither heaven nor hell.

Imagine that.

✦ ✦ ✦

A few years ago *Rolling Stone* magazine polled a select group of recording-industry professionals, critics, and artists, and they ranked "Imagine" the third-greatest song of all time.

In the video for the song, John plays a white grand piano in a white room. His wife, Yoko Ono, walks around the room, throwing open the curtains on all the windows, one by one. When I saw the video, I wanted to shout: *No! She should be closing the curtains! The song isn't enlightening anything. It's a deepening darkness.*

It only got deeper. A few years later Bob Dylan was "born again" and outed himself with his hit single "Gotta Serve Somebody." You probably know the song.

> You might be a rock and roll addict prancing on the
>   stage.
> You might have drugs at your command, women in a
>   cage.
> You may be a businessman or some high-degree thief.
> They may call you Doctor or they may call you Chief.
>
> But you're gonna have to serve somebody, yes indeed.
> You're gonna have to serve somebody.
> Well, it may be the devil or it may be the Lord,
> But you're gonna have to serve somebody.[2]

Dylan had been one of Lennon's heroes and an icon of the sixties counterculture. To John, and to a lot of other true believers, such a conversion was unimaginable. They treated it like an apostasy. Dylan had dared to utter heresy and leave the Church of Untrammeled Freedom and Self-worship.

John went into the studio and vented his rage into a long, long song called "Serve Yourself." In case the title doesn't say it all for you, here's a sampling of the lyrics. I'm sure you can find the rest online.

> You say you found Jesus. Christ!
> He's the only one …
> Well there's somethin' missing in this God Almighty
> stew…
> You got to serve yourself.
> Nobody gonna do for you…
> Well you may believe in devils and you may believe in
> laws,
> but if you don't go out and serve yourself, ain't no room
> service here.[3]

Maybe it's not fair to hold John accountable for this. It was just a demo tape, and the poor guy was shot to death shortly after he recorded it. He never had a chance to refine his thoughts.

But then again, John was the great advocate of spontaneous art and primal screams. So maybe he himself has given us a right to respond to his anti-Dylan, anti-Jesus rambling.

John wanted good things. "All you need is love." "Give peace a chance." The problem is that those things slip away like eels unless you have a clear idea of what they are. How could John preach love to the world when he had a hard enough time showing love to the people closest to him? What right did he have to preach world peace when he couldn't even get along with the Beatles?

The Jesus Dylan embraced teaches the way: It's a way of self-sacrificing, self-giving love. It's a way of forgiveness. It's a peace that surpasses all understanding.

Peace isn't the chaos of liberty, anarchy, and license. It is, as St. Augustine said, "tranquility of order."[4] It's the train on the track ("Slow Train Coming," as Dylan put it).

It's good to want a revolution, and it's good to give peace a chance, but the only true revolution that produces lasting peace is the one that Jesus started. The alternatives just make you pick sides among the warring factions. So John ended up throwing his support behind armed terrorists in the IRA and Black Panthers, even though they really weren't interested in giving peace a chance.

The man said it well himself:

> You say you want a revolution.
> Well, you know,
> we all want to change the world....
> You say you'll change the constitution.
> Well, you know,
> you better free your mind instead.[5]

I miss John Lennon. I remember an interview he did with the Canadian Broadcasting Corporation in 1969, in which he said he was "one of Christ's biggest fans."[6] I take that as grounds for hope, and I pray that, through Jesus' abundant mercy, he rests in true peace and knows the love that's "all you need."[7]

13 BRONX IN BLUE

THE BIGGEST HIT OF MY gospel years was "I Put Away My Idols." I wrote it in Israel on pilgrimage. I was reading the book of the prophet Isaiah and thinking about my life. Isaiah said to the people of Israel: "Turn to him from whom you have deeply revolted.... For in that day every one shall cast away his idols of silver and his idols of gold, which your hands have sinfully made for you" (Isaiah 31:6–7).

Was that guy talking about me and my guitar, or what? I had "deeply revolted" all right, and made idols of my gold records.

Looking out on Israel's sands, I started jotting in my notebook. It came out a song.

> I was raised on New York rock and roll.
> I took control.
> I was cool.
> Made the rounds, made the record hops.
> I hit the top,
> played the fool

...

I was living by my horoscope,
taking pills to cope
with my pain.
Rock n roll was my identity,
my whole security.
I made a name.
From above I truly heard a friend:
"Truly now you must be born again."
I put away my idols.
I stripped away all the titles.
Money wrinkles, and things do decay.
I put away my idols.[1]

Almost as soon as I stripped away my titles, God gave them back to me. The album *I Put Away My Idols* was nominated for a Grammy.

As a serious Christian and a serious rocker, I felt at first like a stranger in a strange land. I wasn't sure how I was supposed to be. But others emerged: Paul Stookey, of Peter, Paul, and Mary, Richie Furay of Buffalo Springfield and Poco. Richie even entered the ministry and became quite a preacher and teacher. Then came all the Jesus Rock, and you could hear praise even on the rock radio stations.

* * *

I recorded five gospel albums. I toured churches playing my new songs. And I still did gigs playing my old hits. I stayed constant with my old musical passions.

Little Steven Van Zandt likes to tell a story about his first encounter with me. It was long before he became "Miami

Steve" of Bruce Springsteen's E Street Band (and a star of TV's "The Sopranos"). He was just a kid who had picked up a touring gig with the Dovells, and they had come to Las Vegas. He was enjoying the time listening to many of the rock heroes from his childhood (in the very recent past).

He showed up for my sound check at the Flamingo, and he was lurking in the back. He must have expected me to do something smooth and doo-wop—or maybe a verse of "Where or When." I shocked him when I let loose with Robert Johnson's "Walkin' Blues" on my guitar. It made him grab his own instrument, a Fender Stratocaster, and come up to join in. (We've been close ever since.)

The gospel tunes expressed something important in my life. The old hits were still a joy. But the blues were my natural default. It's what I played when I was playing for myself or friends. For years people who knew me well urged me to put out a blues album. Bonnie Raitt did, and so did Van Morrison.

I resisted the idea. After all, how do you square the apparent despair of the blues with the joy and hope of a Christian?

I should have known better. Years before I'd had the pleasure of visiting the blind bluesman Reverend Gary Davis in his home, talking with him and listening as he (and his guitar) cried out to Jesus.

In 1964 I went to the Newport Folk Festival because some of my friends were playing, and some of my heroes. That's where I first met another great bluesman, Skip James. We talked about the blues, guitars, Jesus, and his health. He was one beautiful, shy, mysterious dude, who sang as if he was from outer space. Mississippi John Hurt sat quietly smiling while we talked.

Their work and quiet Christian witness should have been enough for me. But God often needs to do extraordinary things to get through to me. And one of those times he gave me the blues.

I was on a plane flying home from the West Coast and feeling restless, so I wandered up to the magazine rack to get myself something to read. The thing that caught my eye was the Bible, so I grabbed it and took it back to my seat. I opened the book at random and landed on the book of Psalms. I just started reading—and I couldn't stop. I guess I'd never read the Psalms all in a row like that. But it struck me: Those songs from three thousand years ago, they were the blues.

> My soul is sorely troubled.
> But, O Lord—how long? …
> I'm weary with my moaning;
> at night I flood my bed with tears;
> I drench my couch with weeping.
> My eyes waste away with grief.
> I'm worn down by all my foes.
> (Psalm 6:3, 6–7, with some slight liberties taken)

Man! Sing it, David! I mean, can't you just hear the guy letting loose on his harp in between lines like those?

My buddy Scott Hahn, the Bible scholar, likes to point out that the Psalter has more songs of complaint than any other kind of song. Complaining, he says, is different from grumbling. The Israelites grumbled in the desert, to each other. David complained—to God. We complain to someone we trust. Old King David wasn't just kvetching; he was complaining to a Father. He was singing the blues.

As I kept reading in the Psalms, my brain felt as if it was going to explode. It was all coming together for me. If I'd had my guitar, I probably would have stood on the seat and wailed to the entire airplane. (Ah, the days before Homeland Security.) Never before had I known the blues this way—at least not consciously. Never before had I known the blues the way Gary Davis and Skip James had. This was a gift, a grace from God.

I came to define the blues as "the naked cry of the human heart longing to be in union with God." That's what it was for the greatest bluesmen, whether they knew it or not, and many of them knew it. God gave us the blues because he knew that, without the form, we'd explode from our suffering.

When I sing the blues, I can express my joys, sorrows, fears, and hope. It's a place where a singer can be totally honest on the journey home—get it all out so it doesn't get twisted up inside. It feels so good to sing about something that hurts so bad.

* * *

Well, when Bonnie Raitt and Van Morrison say you should do something, you take it seriously. But my experience on the plane was a calling of an altogether different order. Now I hungered to do that album.

When I laid down the tracks for *Bronx in Blue*, it was me and my guitar and not much else. Some friends added some spare, quiet drumming. But I wanted it to feel genuine, rootsy. I wanted it to be me too. So it's got the sound of Bronx soul. I had some fun with the form.

People sometimes cluck about the blues because of its innuendo and frankly randy sexuality. I tried turning the whole thing upside down. I wrote a blues tune that celebrates monogamy and married love, and it became one of the best-received songs on the album.

> They call me Sweet Papa D
> cos I'm slammin' and tall.
> But when it comes time to get my ashes hauled,
> I let my baby do that.
> I let my baby do that.
> I let my baby do that, and it ease my worried mind.
> I got a red Corvette and I got a strict rule:
> When it gets too hot, I want my engine cooled.
> I let my baby do that.
> I let my baby do that.
> I let my baby do that, and it ease my worried mind.[2]

It may say more than we'd want to say in prime time, but so does the theology of the body. It speaks faithful love in a manly key, and I think it would ring the bell for any bluesman.

It rang the bell for the critics anyway. "Bronx in Blue" got a Grammy nomination in 2008. So now I've been nominated in three genres: rock, gospel, and blues. Not bad for a kid from Belmont Avenue.

13 BRONX IN BLUE

14 GETTING TO THE ESSENTIALS

15 I ROME AROUND

I NEVER GOT MUCH INTO the "denominational" mind-set when I was an evangelical Christian. To most members of most (maybe all) of the churches I attended, the label didn't make much of a difference. I tended to go where I found loud volume and exuberance. I equated that with confidence, which I further equated with truth.

I'd be chugging along at one place, and then I'd hear about someplace new—a plain storefront in a shopping center, where some new preacher was belting it out with a new vitality. So on the next Sunday, I'd drag Susan along, talking up the place all the way in the car. We'd arrive to a room with linoleum and folding chairs. And Susan—who had seen St. Peter's in Rome with me—would say, in her beautiful Bronx deadpan: "I wonder what this place will look like in two thousand years."

We moved house a few times, and that led to more switches in membership. My touring exposed me to many other churches. When I got to a place, I wouldn't just do the gospel show. I'd also attend the sponsoring church's Bible study if one was available.

I met a lot of wonderful people, but I started to notice that we, meaning we Christians, seemed to believe many different and contradictory things. Baptists believed in free will, but Calvinists didn't. Lutherans believed Jesus was truly present in the Eucharist, but evangelicals didn't and rarely celebrated the Lord's Supper. Episcopalians put a lot of stock in their hierarchy (bishops, priests, and deacons), while Baptists prided themselves on not having any. And on infant baptism, everybody was all over the doctrinal map.

That's just a small sampling of a wide range of issues, doctrinal and practical. How could I rejoice in having the truth when I couldn't say for certain what that truth was—couldn't put a line of it into propositional form without starting a holy war?

When I brought this up, people would tell me not to worry: All that mattered was that I was saved. But you know what, you can't get a roomful of American Christians to come to a decent agreement about what it means to be saved or to stay saved.

∘ ∘ ∘

The more people minimized the doctrinal differences, the more I became alarmed. Every Sunday we attended worship services that were almost entirely made up of preaching. Some man was interpreting the Bible for us, giving us doctrine. But what qualified him to do it? If he was genuinely qualified by an anointing of the Holy Spirit, and there is only one Holy Spirit, why couldn't I get two of these guys to agree about their interpretations? If there is "one Lord, one faith, one baptism" (Ephesians 4:5), why were there tens of thousands of denominations, many of them (at least officially) believing that all the others were heretics to some degree?

I took these questions to my pastors, and—God bless them—they took me seriously. They gave me time.

One man, a Presbyterian pastor for whom I have profound love and great respect, listened to me patiently and responded with a saying he had obviously committed to memory: "Unity in the essentials; liberty in the non-essentials; and charity in all things."

Wow! I asked him to repeat it while I wrote it down.

He did, and then added, "That's Augustine."

So I pondered that saying over the next few days, and I went looking for books by this Augustine character. I read his *Confessions* and discovered that he and I had some things in common—like juvenile delinquency!

I read more, and something started to bother me. The Church Augustine described didn't look much like the place I went to on Sundays. He talked about the Mass and the real presence. He talked about Rome's authority. ("Rome has spoken," he said. "The matter is settled."[1]) He preached about the saints. What's more, he talked about these things as "essentials" and not at all optional. What was going on here?

How could the pastor accept the truth of that statement of Augustine and yet apply it to a different (and sometimes opposite) set of beliefs? If Augustine was right, then which doctrines were essentials? The Trinity? The divinity of Christ? Salvation by faith alone? The frequent observance of the Lord's Supper? I could drive around my city for a day and find pastors to oppose one another on matters that looked to me like core dogmas.

✵ ✵ ✵

For the first time in my life as a Christian, I was facing a crisis of faith. So I did what I had been taught to do. I went to the Bible. But even there the teaching didn't seem to match up with what we were practicing and preaching in our storefront missions. "First of all you must understand this, that no prophecy of scripture is a matter of one's own interpretation" (2 Peter 1:20). Well, that one alone pulled the rug out from under my experience of denominational Christianity!

"If I should be delayed, you should know how to behave in the household of God, which is the church of the living God, the pillar and foundation of the truth" (1 Timothy 3:15, *NAB*). Uh, yeah, St. Paul, but which Church and which truth?

In the midst of all this, Susan and I were invited to a Christmas party at a local Catholic church. It was just a social gathering. It was the parish of some friends of ours, and they invited us along. I didn't remember much about Catholicism from my childhood catechism classes. In fact, I had spent a lot more time studying anti-Catholicism, and that was more consti-tutional to me.

The people at the party must have figured I was Catholic, with a name like DiMucci, so they spoke openly. They were having a discussion about the practice of closed Communion and why the Church restricted the sacrament to professing believers who were in the state of grace. I was impressed. Not only were they describing the Church as I found it in Augustine, but they were describing the Church as I found it in St. Paul (in 1 Corinthians 10—11). This seemed to jibe, for me, with what Jesus was saying in his long discourse in the sixth chapter of John's Gospel, where he's preaching so urgently and forcefully about the centrality of the Eucharist. What part of

"This is my body" don't you understand?

As I thought about it, it seemed that the newer a denomination was, the less seriously it took Jesus' teaching on this obviously essential matter; the less they wanted to "do this" in remembrance of him. These Catholics took Jesus at his word, and they believed the Eucharist was his Body, Blood, Soul, and Divinity. And they acted accordingly—with closed Communion, reverence for their tabernacle, an obligation to attend Mass, and many other doctrines and practices.

The Eucharist was the fixed point in a changing world. It was the principle of unity and truth, because "it" was a "he," and he was Jesus. "Because there is one bread, we who are many are one body, for we all partake of the one bread" (1 Corinthians 10:17).

I didn't like where my thoughts were heading. If these conclusions were right, it would mean that I had been wrong about many things. And I've never been warm to that conclusion.

Believe it or not, that night I went home and got quiet. I sat in front of the TV and picked up the remote. I was up for a distraction.

So I started channel surfing, and I landed on this show with two talking heads, and one guy was talking about how he had been an Episcopalian minister, and he faced a crisis of faith that sounded similar to mine (though he was a lot smarter). He said that the basic problem was authority. Everybody was in rebellion. Nobody wanted to acknowledge there was authority on earth. So he found himself in the middle of a constant riot of interpretations.

So he became a Catholic. It said on the TV screen that his name was Dr. John Haas, and he was a bioethicist. The man interviewing him was named Marcus Grodi, and he had been a Presbyterian minister before he, too, became Catholic.

Authority. That's it, I thought. This Catholic guy nailed it. We were all in rebellion. And we were in rebellion against the very Church that had put the New Testament together in one book—in the lifetime of St. Augustine.

✤ ✤ ✤

I started watching that channel a lot more: the Eternal Word Television Network. And I started reading Catholic books, and I started reading the ancient Fathers, like Augustine. They spoke to something deep inside me, a yearning to get back to the roots.

When it came to music, I was always drawn back to the beginnings: the early bluesmen.

When it came to my love for America, I was always drawn back to the founders: Washington, Jefferson, Hamilton. Even when it came to understanding my own sobriety, I threw myself back upon the early sources, the writings of the founders of the twelve-step movement.

In every aspect of life, I observed and respected a kind of "apostolic succession," so why not in religion? I read the earliest Church fathers, the ones who knew the authors of the New Testament, the ones who had been ordained by the apostles, and—you know what?—they taught me the Good Book with a good Catholic eye.

Next time I was in New York, I knew what I had to do.

I took a cab to Belmont Avenue in the Bronx, and I went to Mount Carmel Church. I buzzed the rectory and asked the priest, Fr. Frank, if he would hear my confession. (Msgr. Pernicone had long since gone to his reward.)

Of course he obliged. We went over to the confessional, sat down, and I said to him, "Fr. Frank, I feel like I've been persecuting Christ, the body of Christ, the Church. I didn't know…"

He stopped me in my tracks. "Dion," he said, "stand up."

I stood up. And he hugged me. And he said, "Welcome home."

15 I ROME AROUND

A FEW TIMES IN THE course of this book, I've mentioned that I have a prejudice against Italians. Now, to you maybe that sounds absurd, but for me it was real.

Mid-century was an awkward time for Italians. We were trying to make it in the New World. But we were still vying for status according to our Old World standards. Our neighborhoods operated on the assumption that the goal in life was to get out of the neighborhood, to be assimilated, to look "American." Yet we still had mafioso wannabes who thought their pin-striped suits and hundred-dollar bills would win them "respect" (meaning fear). I got out as soon as I could.

To me it was richly ironic that some critics cited me as an example of an emerging movement they called "ethnic rock." Whatever. If people wanted to buy my records just because I had Italian blood, that was fine by me.

In Italy, I learned, the folks were proud of me. The country's defeat in World War II was still a fresh memory. Yet here was one of "theirs," a DiMucci, making it big in American pop music.

I was invited to Italy and given the grand tour. Someone translated my song "Donna the Prima Donna" into Italian—and though I couldn't understand a word of it, I sang it with gusto, and it soared to the top of the Italian charts. (I later found out that the translator had changed the story line significantly and introduced a lecherous bill collector into the mix. I had no idea what I was singing.)

In Italy I encountered Italian culture, not just the faint echo I'd heard in America. I met the people, heard the poetry, attended the opera, saw the art. I learned that there was so much more to it than we had been able to fit in our trunks when we came to America. And I fell in love with it all.

◦ ◦ ◦

Susan was with me—God bless her for her patience—and I insisted on taking her through every museum, every monument, and every church that housed a masterpiece. I was her self-appointed tour guide, and I paced her through the master-works, just as my father used to take me through the Museum of Modern Art when I was a kid. I pointed out the subtleties in the sculpture and paintings, the strokes of genius, the illusions in the architecture. I held forth on the vision of the artists. It was all about self-expression, technique.

In Italian culture, as in my life, art was supreme, and the artist was godlike as he created.

Some years passed before our next trip to Italy, and by then I had become a Christian. Susan was with me—God bless her—and again I put her through the paces.

But it was different now. It was all about the glory of God. The statues and paintings brought out the small details of the biblical stories, the nuances of the characters in the Exodus, the drama of the Gospels, the foibles of the apostles. Now, for me, the artworks were sermons to be absorbed through the eyes (Susan, are you listening?) but pondered in the soul.

The third time's a charm. After I'd returned to the practice of the Catholic faith, Susan and I made another trip to Rome. And you know what? This time I managed to shut up. I was in awe. As I stepped out in that eternal city, I finally began to see why Rome mattered so much. It was the end point of the Acts of the Apostles. All Peter's trials, all Paul's travels—all roads led to Rome. Paul's most important letter was addressed to the Christians of Rome. Other letters had Rome as the return address. It was the ground in Rome that soaked up the blood of the apostles, Peter and Paul, and made that place a holy city.

I was no longer a tourist. I was a pilgrim. But I was home too, in some sense. And I confess: I was more than a little proud to be Italian.

✵ ✵ ✵

Susan and I still live in Florida, but we keep a small efficiency apartment in New York City. It's our base of operations when I'm touring every year.

A block away from that place is the grave of the patriot Alexander Hamilton, one of the founders of our country, and I love to read his epitaph: "The patriot of incorruptible integrity, the soldier of approved valor, the statesman of consummate wisdom, whose talents and virtue will be admired by grateful posterity long after this marble shall have moldered into dust."

If that's true of Hamilton—and of course it is!—how much more true of St. Peter and St. Paul?

16 HANGING OUT WITH THE SAINTS

DOCTORS OFTEN COUNSEL THEIR PATIENTS to be patient. Healing takes time. But we give in to the temptation and lift the bandage and peek. We see the scar and wonder what's taking so long.

The Divine Physician healed some things instantly for me—my obsession with drink and drugs. But other things, he knew in his wisdom, were best left to time.

My father and I had a difficult and conflicted relationship. He was my hero. He was, for me, the model of the artist's mind and the artist's approach to reality. Yet he had also abdicated his most important roles in our family. He was never a provider or moral guide. He had failed me, I thought, precisely as a father.

I remember one day when I was touring to promote "Abraham, Martin, and John," I was playing a college in Michigan, and this kid came up to me after the show and asked for an autograph. Then he kind of nervously asked for another, "for my dad…he's a fan of yours, and he's coming to visit me this weekend.… You know how dads are."

113

I laughed as if I understood, and I signed the second auto-graph, but I had no idea what that kid was talking about—and I felt his words like a knife between my ribs.

In his old age my father lived near me in Florida. Still living on health food, still working out, he used to swim in the canals with the alligators.

* * *

My father was ninety-one and still healthy as a racehorse in its prime. I remember one day we were walking together and talk-ing about the past, and I guess something inside me wanted to lead him to an apology. I asked him some leading questions. I asked if there was anything he regretted in his life.

He said, "No, not a thing"—and it hit me like a punch in the gut. Not only did this guy opt out of any significant role in my upbringing—but he'd do it all the same way if he were given another chance. I didn't know what to say. I was struck dumb. (Take a moment and savor that. It doesn't happen too often.)

It took me a while to formulate another thought and then another question, this one more pointed. "Would you do *any-thing* differently if you could?"

He was quiet for a while, and then he said, "I'd spend more time with my brother. I miss him now."

I couldn't believe the man was saying this to his son. He must have seen I was hot under the collar—and it wasn't the Florida humidity.

"Dion," he said, and he looked me right in the eye, "a man becomes exactly the person he wants to become."

And then he left. And he left me to ponder that line.

* * *

We all become the person we want to become. You know, he was right. But I'd make a slight adjustment, an addition: *We all become the person we want to become—given what we know.*

It seems to me that life—real life, the way God made it to be—is like a banquet, with all the sumptuous foods an army of Italian grandmothers could put together. Yet some people never go into the banquet hall. Instead they stop in the waiting room because there's a big bowl of Cheetos and a bottle of Diet Pepsi. Don't get me wrong: I like Cheetos and Diet Pepsi. But let's talk sense here.

My dad never knew there was a supernatural feast going on, so he sat there gorging himself on natural pleasures. He became exactly who he wanted to be.

For you and me though, it's different. Once we know Jesus Christ, the game changes. We want to have "the mind of Christ" (1 Corinthians 2:16) more perfectly every day. We won't be happy just settling for three squares and a warm bed. We want to have his mind for our own. We want to have God's nature for our own (see 2 Peter 1:4). We want to suffer with his body, not our own (see Colossians 1:4).

I think I came to a deeper understanding of the situation that day, but I didn't really get closure. And it wasn't long afterward, on August 21, 2003, that Pasquale DiMucci, my father, died. It was sudden. One day he was healthy. Next day he fell over.

My mother said, in her inimitable way, "A lot of good health food does you. He's dead, and I'm alive. All that walking! Eating seaweed! Ha! Bunch of malarkey."

❊ ❊ ❊

Grief is a strange thing. My father was gone. I was a Christian. Those circumstances should have been good enough for me to get over it and move on. But I couldn't. I'd be out running errands, thinking about something mundane, when suddenly I'd be filled with furious anger toward the guy.

It was still preoccupying me in midyear 2005 as I prepared to make a pilgrimage to Rome with the St. Paul Center for Biblical Theology. I went with a group of about a hundred people, and Dr. Scott Hahn led us on a relentless and relentlessly cheerful march through all the ancient sites: St. Peter's, St. Paul's, St. John Lateran, the holy stairs, the Colosseum, the Forum. Even though I'd been to Rome several times before, I learned so much. Scott carries a library of biblical studies, history, and theology in his brain, and he shares it in a genial and generous way.

I was impressed also by the center's chaplain, Fr. Joseph Linck. He was a quiet, bashful, scholarly guy, in his early thirties, with wire-rimmed glasses and a receding hairline. (Both are marks of distinction in my book.) From table talk in the restaurants where we ate, I concluded that Fr. Joe was brilliant. He was an historian, a scholar of American Church history but also of the early Church fathers. He wore his brilliance lightly and spoke with a quiet wit. In the pulpit he turned into a lion—the man could preach the Word with the best—though in the confessional he was the Lamb.

Rome was suffering that summer through record heat and record humidity. By midday we pilgrims were swimming in our own sweat and only too happy to duck into the historic churches. The temperature dropped a good ten degrees when I stepped into the Church of St. Peter in Chains. Our group shuffled along slowly toward the place where the apostle's chains were kept for veneration. My turn came, and I don't know how to describe what happened to me.

Kneeling before those chains, some strong chains on my heart were broken. I started sobbing uncontrollably but with utter joy, and all I could think about was my father, Pasquale DiMucci.

I stepped out of the church and into the sun, and there was Fr. Joe, sitting in the little piazza. I walked up to him and said, "Can you please explain what just happened to me?"

He said he'd try. So I told him.

He smiled. The man was just a kid, but he spoke with the wisdom of years. He said, "Dion, relationships don't end."

✿ ✿ ✿

I had never heard anything like that. He went on: "Dion, be open to all the grace God wants to give while you're here. Your father wasn't open to grace in his life. So you need to be open and pray for him, pray for his soul, pray for his rest. Where he is, he may be praying for you. You'll be helping each other."

He brought the communion of saints down to just hanging out. That changed my life. Through the rest of the pilgrimage —and the rest of my days—I was under obligation to reconnect: with Buddy Holly, Big Bopper, Ritchie Valens, Sam Cooke.

"Relationships don't end." That's what the Church prays in the Mass of Christian Burial: "Lord, for Your faithful people life is changed not ended." Ah, now I see.

I have not been angry with my father since that day. God is merciful. "And he will turn the hearts of fathers to their children and the hearts of children to their fathers" (Malachi 4:6).

That event in Rome broke me down. God went into a place in my head that I could never get to. And he went there and threw the switch, and I realized that my father was my hero, in spite of how imperfect he was and what I expected from him.

My relationship with Fr. Joe hasn't ended either, though cancer took him, quite young and quite suddenly, not long after that day in Rome.

17 DREAMS

THE FUNNY THING ABOUT DREAMS is that sometimes they come true. And sometimes the way they come true is pretty funny.

The year was 2006, and I was sitting in Café Milano, a great Italian restaurant in Washington, D.C., at a dinner sponsored by the National Italian-American Foundation (NIAF). I like what the organization does. It's an educational foundation that promotes Italian American culture and heritage. It also fights discrimination and harmful stereotypes in the media. When they ask me to do something, I'm eager to help, and I'm usually star struck by the company I keep.

That night I watched many celebrities stroll into the elegant dining room and be ushered to their assigned seats: Rudy Giuliani, Nancy Pelosi, Martin Scorsese, Yogi Berra, Justices Antonin Scalia and Samuel Alito, Susan Lucci, Tony LoBianco, Dick Vermeil, and Jerry Vale, to name just a few.

A young man escorted a beautiful and elegant lady to the seat beside me. She bore herself so gracefully, with just a touch of aloofness. I thought she must be a countess or a queen. What can a rock and roller from the Bronx have to say to royalty? I was afraid I might have a long and awkward evening ahead of me.

But she immediately dispelled my fears by launching into conversation—even before we'd had a chance to be properly introduced. After just a few sentences in her poetically accented English, I knew who she was. Gina Lollobrigida.

When I was growing up in the 1950s in my Italian neighborhood in the Bronx, Gina Lollobrigida was the ideal of feminine beauty for my friends and me. Her nickname in the papers was "the World's Most Beautiful Woman," after the title of one of her movies. Not long off the boat from Subiaco, she was darkhaired, dark-eyed, and charming in every way.

In 2006 she still was all of that. And suddenly I was a teenager again.

I repeated her name, out loud, slowly, "Gina Lollobrigida," and I laughed as I confessed to her: "You know, when I was fifteen I had two fantasies: one, to own a Martin D-28 guitar, just like Hank Williams played. The other was to have a date with Gina Lollobrigida.

"Well, I got the Martin guitar a long time ago. If you'll let me call this a date, then all my dreams will have come true!"

She accepted those terms, and so my long-ago aspirations were fulfilled. We enjoyed our dinner and conversation.

"When I was a child," says St. Paul, "I spoke like a child, I thought like a child, I reasoned like a child" (1 Corinthians 13:11). I dreamed like a child.

The apostle wasn't talking about any teenage crush when he wrote those words. He was talking about Love with a capital *L*, and that Love is not a something but a Someone. When we dream of lesser loves, even when we're just kids at the movies, it's really the big Love that we're longing for. All the loves along the way teach us, train us, and strengthen us for the only love that lasts.

That's what earthly loves are built to do. They prepare us for God's love. They prepare us for the God who is Love. Sometimes they do it by making us wait for a long time; they stretch our hearts and increase our capacity to give and receive. Sometimes they do it by breaking our hearts, so God can give us a new one.

Love is not just the stuff of daydreams and sighing. It's going back to school.

And we learn along the way that love is all about sacrifice—sacrificing myself for the sake of the one I love. Love is a school of sacrifice, where we learn how to be like Jesus, because sacrifice is the essence of his life. He gave himself up for the one he loved, and that one is you. That one is me.

Go read the Letter to the Hebrews. Jesus is the great high priest of the new covenant, and he offers everything he's got to God the Father. He's a priest, and so he offers a sacrifice.

That's love. Our dreams of love draw us out of ourselves, first maybe when we're teenagers and we see a lovely person like Gina Lollobrigida on the silver screen. We dream of a date, but it's still a dream of getting, and the object remains an object, like a Martin guitar, only better.

But love insists on schooling us, if we'll let it. Through marriage and parenting and even deep friendship, we grow until that lower-case love goes capital on us. Sometimes it happens slowly, with progress you hardly notice. Sometimes it happens suddenly, because of some great shock, or some great joy, or even the sudden intervention of Jesus in your life. (I've had my share of all three.)

We learn to offer ourselves for the sake of someone else, just as Jesus did. Maybe it seems at first that it's not going to be pleasant. We don't want to give. We want to get something out of love. But we learn over time that sacrifice is the only way to happiness.

My studies in love have been true learning experiences, as I've been schooled by the best through more than fifty years of marriage—by my wife, Susan (my real teenage sweetheart, as opposed to my celluloid fantasy). I can't say I've always been a good student. I can't say the material comes easy to me. This I can say: Dreams come true. Prayers are answered. God is good.

And I'm not just talking about classic guitars or dates with starlets.

⓲ TRUTH DECAY

I LOVE THE FOLKS AT the National Italian-American Foundation. The more I think about it, the more dreams I find they've fulfilled, and the more they've given me cause to smile—and occasions to laugh out loud.

Before there was Gina Lollobrigida, I knew another graceful presence. To a very small boy, girls aren't particularly important. Neither are movies. But baseball—*baseball*, as the saying goes—*is life*.

I grew up in the shadow of Yankee Stadium, and like every kid in the neighborhood, I dreamed of one day meeting Joe DiMaggio. He was Italian American like us. He dominated the American League with his steady play. His fifty-six-game hitting streak is a record that still stands.

Sure enough, fast-forward through the decades, and I did get to meet him, at one of those events for Italian Americans. That was memorable, but not half as memorable as another, more recent event.

The organization was honoring the movie director Martin Scorsese, a man I truly admire and respect. He's a great artist, a fellow New Yorker, and a beautiful man in many ways. Scorsese had the microphone, and he said he wanted to use the occasion to pay tribute to Jack Valenti, a former NIAF president who had recently died. I thought that was really cool. I had long admired Jack, who was a dedicated Catholic, well loved by people who knew him.

As Scorsese went on with his "tribute," he quoted often from our departed friend, but his supposed quotations sounded strangely anti-Christian—not the kind of things I could imagine Jack Valenti ever saying. I'm sure Scorsese was still smarting because Christians had roundly condemned his movie *The Last Temptation of Christ* as blasphemous. His eulogy, it seems to me, was occasion for payback. The gist of his ranting was this: Anyone who says he knows the truth is arrogant and deceived. If you meet someone who says he has the truth, run in the other direction. An insistence on truth is fanaticism, plain and simple. There is no objective truth. There is no truth.

I leaned over to Yogi Berra, who was sitting next to me, and I whispered, "Is that *true*?"

Yogi—another baseball hero from my childhood—smiled knowingly and winked.

Many years ago Dorothy Parker observed: "Authors and actors and artists and such / Never know nothing, and never know much."[1]

Of course, if truth doesn't exist, there isn't much to know, is there?

And yet I have very intelligent friends who *know for certain* that nothing whatsoever can be known with certainty. They'll state absolutely that there are no absolutes. They judge it morally wrong to make judgments between right and wrong. Their one dogma is that dogma is forbidden.

And if you try to raise objections to any of this, they'll smile at your childish simplicity.

They think that reality is something that can be manipulated, the way a guitarist bends a note by pressing the string across the fret board. And as a musician, I kind of know what they're getting at. I know that a blue note isn't going to match anything that shows up on sheet music—not truly anyway. But that doesn't mean those notes aren't true as you hear them; nor does it mean the sheet music is lying. It means they're much more than the squiggly lines you see on the page can convey. They correspond, somewhat, to something on the page, but even more to something in the soul, something that's alive. Try substituting for them, and you'll see how true they are.

For music to be free—as it needs to be in rock and roll—you need a sure foundation. You need a certain order. Music has its own kind of truth. If four guitarists with no training get in a room and start hitting randomly on the strings—without knowing the scales, the harmonics, the key, the tempo, or the structure of the song—you'll have total chaos. The seven-tone scale makes a lot of things possible. Believe in its truth, and you find a variety of free expression and individuality, from Chuck Berry and John Lee Hooker to Jimi Hendrix and Les Paul.

The older I get, the more I'm knocked out by the glory of the truth. We can't comprehend it, but we can know it, because the truth has been revealed, and it corresponds to what we know from our senses and the right use of our reason. Some people who are wise by worldly standards say they can't see it anymore (but just watch out when they think they've been wronged). Still, it's plain as day to little children and to ordinary Christians with good common sense.

When you set yourself against the truth, you might get more pleasure out of the world, but you find yourself less happy. You can afford to get your kicks where you want them; but then, after a while, you're not really having your kicks. They're having you. They own you. And you're not happy at all. Neither are your kids or your several successive spouses.

You've moved far from your life's center, and you're miserable. The truth hasn't moved at all, and the people who have stayed close to it are happy, and so are their families. They *know* the truth, and the truth sets them *free*. There's nothing fanatical about them. They're truly free.

The truth can be known and wants to be known. It's steadier than my beloved Bronx Bomber, Joltin' Joe. It's way more permanent than his record-hitting streak. And like the streak, it seems to be unapproachable. Except it's not.

In fact, the truth comes to approach us. It comes to us in the gospel. It comes to us in the Mass.

But to get back to Martin Scorsese's dinner speech: It took place on a Saturday night, so the next big event was Sunday Mass. Early the next day I made my way down to the lobby of the Hilton, where an Italian-American bishop was offering Mass for our group. As I got off the elevator and strolled across the lobby, I saw Yogi there—in his Sunday best, headed for Mass. And so I joined him once again.

Though Yogi grew up in St. Louis and I grew up in the Bronx, we were both at home when we got to the hotel's makeshift altar and sanctuary. That's what it means to be Catholic. That's where we find our center—at the altar, where heaven touches down to earth with the thud of the truth. It may be in St. Peter's, or it may be in a hotel, but heaven touches down with the same thud—and sounds out with the ring of truth.

And you'll never guess what Gospel the bishop preached to us. There was Jesus himself telling us about objective truth. Truth you can know. Truth that wants to be known. Jesus said that Sunday, "I am the way, and the truth, and the life" (John 14:6).

I looked again at Yogi, and again he smiled back at me, knowingly, and winked.

19 TWO LETTERS TO JAMES

I'VE CHANGED THE NAME OF the recipient, but these are real letters I wrote to someone I love.

Dear James,

I am a ferocious Catholic who loves the Church and its teaching. But I truly believe that few people who call themselves Catholic or Christian have ever consciously asked God to fill them with his Holy Spirit or made a decision to follow Jesus Christ. Maybe they hang on because of habit or status or for some other reason. Maybe it's just stubborn grace. Maybe, too, they're on their way and don't know it yet. The Church strives to keep everyone close and doesn't judge anyone's heart. You'll find many people canonized as saints but no one publicly damned—not even criminals like Jeffrey Dahmer. The novelist James Joyce called the Catholic Church "Here Comes Everybody," and that's what I like about it. No one's turned away because of race or ethnicity, ability or disability. No one's turned away because of sin. There's even room for me.

I came home to the Church many years ago, by the grace of God. But I came for good reasons. It works. It's true.

Albert Einstein made his breakthroughs in physics. They worked, and they continue to work. People who know physics tell me they do, and so I accept his authority on their authority, and because they've judged the proof. It's the same way with the breakthroughs in medicine I learn about from my doctor. I'm not an M.D., but I trust the authority of the one I hired. It works.

The Son of God came to show us how to live and love. He has the authority. I accept it. The problem is, most people don't. They're trying to reinvent the wheel. I was there, and I know it doesn't work. I used to be outside the Church, screaming, yelling, and kicking it. I discovered that the problems weren't so much with the Church as with me. Even with my problems, and even after I spent all that time kicking at its walls, the Church was willing to take me in and give me a place to work out God's will for me.

There is a truth. You know this, because you've worked with the laws of physics to invent a car that could serve not only you but lots of folks who would otherwise face great limitations. And you've never made a cent off your invention. You couldn't have done that unless you had taken hard, unflinching looks at the truth.

The truth isn't limited to what we can see. You know this too. You have kept a good home and family because you know that kindness operates according to certain laws. The life you live—a life I admire—is a witness that humanity works best when it follows a moral law engraved in our conscience by God himself. Life is beautiful when somebody tells the truth, makes sacrifices for the sake of others, and acts courageously. Cowardice is ugly; so are lies and selfishness. None of this is self-evident. But you know these things are true, and you live that truth better than most people I know.

Maybe you've been turned off to Christianity because some Christians, and even some people who claim to be Christian leaders, promote ideas and practices that you know are untrue or ugly. God forgive them. They don't know what they're doing, because they don't know what they're trying to undo.

The truth isn't a something—it's a somebody, and his name is Jesus. He started a Church, which is the humble servant and custodian of the truth. It made walls so solid that I could actually kick them, back when I wanted to. Nobody else had made anything that mattered that much to me, because nobody else had built something so sturdy as the truth of Jesus Christ. Pope Benedict XVI said relativism is the biggest problem we are facing today—everybody defining their own truth—and I have to agree with him. In a world of squish, the Church stands as something solid.

In spite of everything, James—in spite of scandalous Christians in the public square, in spite of me—the

Church keeps on as something truly beautiful, majestic, and glorious, as something that works because it's true. I pray someday you'll see it and see that it works for you.

Love,

Dion

❦ ❦ ❦

Dear James,

You're right when you say that God's not the problem. Your next line is also true: "It was the people I met who spoke for the Church. People can let you down, God doesn't." It's true, but it needs some unpacking.

It's more accurate, I think, to say that the problem is people, pure and simple. It does sound like you met some doozies, and I regret the things they said and did to you.

But when I take a hard look in the mirror, I walk away knowing that their behavior wasn't much worse than mine was when I was drunk and high. Were they abusive? I was abusive in my own way. Did they treat their family unjustly? Well, I know I did. And I was probably as mean-spirited as any of them. If I had the stomach for it, and if my friends and family were less forgiving than they are, I could probably gather testimonies to make my point.

One of the modern saints once told a cardinal that whenever he recited the creed and professed his belief in the "one holy, catholic, and apostolic Church," he always added the phrase "in spite of everything."

When the cardinal asked him what he meant by that, he said, "I mean your sins and mine."

Catholics have always been realistic about the situation—I mean, about being human. Blaise Pascal was a great scientist, a theoretical statistician, and some people call him the inventor of the computer. He was also a keen observer of human psychology. He decried the corruption in the Church in his own day, and he even wrote satires of it, but he always started with Number One. He always recognized that, more than anyone else, he was the problem.

It's often said that the Church is not so much a hotel for saints as a hospital for sinners. And in sheer numbers that's got to be true. For every Mother Teresa there are a million old Italians like me from the Bronx. For every Damien on Molokai, there are countless Hawaiian Christians who are only out to get lei'd.

The amazing thing is that Damien and Mother Teresa would still greet me as a brother, close kin in our dignity and close kin in our sin. We could belong to the same family. We do belong to the same family even now.

The Church is big, and it has room for everybody. That doesn't mean we're one big, happy family. Remember, I called it a hospital for sinners. Hospitals make people cranky, sad, angry, resentful. They're run by administrators and doctors who aren't always there for the best reasons. Some of them are motivated by greed, or by the desire to have power over others, or even by a real cruel streak. But, you know, when I'm sick, I'd rather be in the hospital than lying on the floor of my bathroom. In the hospital I'm much more likely to get the help I need.

The Church is a big family. Here's the way you and I learned it in catechism class: There's the Church Militant, the Church Suffering, and the Church Triumphant. The Church Militant is struggling here on earth. The Church Suffering is getting washed up in purgatory, because we're all sinners and nothing impure can enter heaven. The Church Triumphant is living in glory in heaven; but because they share God's life, they share his presence with us even now. I get choked up, James, when I think that this quite likely includes some of our family members.

The Church on earth is the part we can see, and what we see can give us indigestion. What you've seen does give me indigestion. But the Church is like a lighthouse. If the lighthouse keeper is a cheating, lying, creepy scoundrel, you don't get rid of the lighthouse. That would be disastrous. When Bill Clinton fell from grace, we didn't give up on democracy or the presidency. When the Yankees have an off year, we don't nuke the franchise or give up on baseball.

For years though, that's what I preferred to do. I let my resentments occupy my mind. I let the villains win, because I let them define the Church for me. They loomed so large for me that I forgot about the people I knew who lived quiet, holy lives of kindness and prayer. I forgot about Mother Teresa's nuns who stayed by the bedside of AIDS patients and addicts who had spent their lives alienating everybody else in the world. Those ladies won't let people die alone as pariahs, even when they've earned it! I forgot about the beautiful things produced by great and devout Catholics: the spirituality of Francis of Assisi, the thoughts of Thomas Aquinas, the music of Mozart, the poetry of Dante, the imaginary world of Tolkien, the scientific rigor of Mendel, Pasteur, Lavoisier, Von Neumann.

The thing I'm trying to do now is connect with that beauty and holy ambition. Those people did what they did—and those good nuns do what they do—because they're doing it for God. They can love despicable sinners because they love God in those despicable sinners. As a recovering despicable sinner, I can appreciate that, and it inspires me to put aside my resentments. It inspires me not to let the bastards win. It inspires me to love the bastards—and to recognize myself as one.

It's a big Church. There's room for me. James, I have to believe there's room for you, because you've lived a better life than I have. You inspire me to do beautiful things and not think so much about myself. I know you think about me, because you're kind. I hope you'll give some thought to what I'm saying.

I'm grateful for all those good people in the Church—Militant, Triumphant, and Suffering. I ignored them for many years while I focused on their less savory coreligionists. But they didn't ignore me. They didn't give up on me. They kept praying for me, quietly witnessing to me and doing good things for me.

When I came back, they were happy to have me for
heaven, even after I had given them hell for years.
Love,
Dion

19 TWO LETTERS TO JAMES

NOTES

20 KING OF THE NEW YORK STREETS

NOW THAT YOU'VE ENDURED NINETEEN chapters of my talking about myself, you're probably dying to hear the title of my next book. Well, I think it's going to be *Humility, and How I Achieved It!*

Rock stars—is there anything we don't know? Is there anything we're not eager to teach the world? Just tune in to *Entertainment Tonight* or pick up a copy of *Rolling Stone*, and there we are, pontificating to a waiting world.

Whenever I get full of myself, I ponder a cartoon my wife keeps in the kitchen. It shows Ludwig von Beethoven sitting at the piano, his hair wild, his whole body in the passionate throes of his genius. His wife is standing off to the side, wearing an apron and holding a broom, saying, "Beethoven...the garbage."

We rock and rollers would have you believe that we know how to put an end to poverty, war, and injustice. Meanwhile, at home we can't seem to remember to take out the trash.

Well, as you've probably guessed by now, I may be a rock star, but there's plenty I don't know. The stories of my life are enough evidence to convict me—or at least get me sent back to high school, though the teachers probably wouldn't want me back! Remember the trouble I caused the last time I was there? They probably keep very good records.

I know this much: The longer I live, the more *I've* been able to love that kid who used to sing and rumble in the streets of the Bronx. I don't excuse the things he did—the things I did. But I'm beginning to understand the kid who did them.

I've had to forgive a lot of people through the years. Most of the time it's been hard to do. But forgiving friends and even adversaries is easier than accepting *the sufficiency of God's forgiveness*—easier than listening with peaceful gratitude when Father pronounces those words of absolution over me in the confessional.

It's hard, but I'm getting there. Writing a book helps too, so I thank you for helping me do it.

Maybe I'm beginning to see that long-ago kid as Msgr. Pernicone saw him, as Sarah Alba did, and as Doc Pomus did.

You know, I was just sixteen years old when I wrote a song that said more than I'd intended:

> I'd like to tell you something
> all about the good and the bad.
> I wish today the world, my friends,
> would stop being sad.
> There's so much evil round us,
> I feel that I could die.
> And I know, yeah,
> that I was born to cry....
> Well, every girl I ever loved

always stepped on my feet.
I thought I had a friend once,
but he kicked out my teeth.
The things I like and wanna have
I can't even buy.
But I know, yeah,
that I was born to cry.
Well, I know someday
and maybe soon
that Master will call,
and when he does,
I'll tell you something,
I won't cry at all.[1]

The kid who wrote that song couldn't have been all bad. He just needed some polish.

OK, maybe a lot of polish.

But I couldn't have written that song better if I'd written it last week. When the Master does come to call, I hope he'll like it, too.

In my later autobiographical songs, I try to understand the kid. I'm thinking especially about "King of the New York Streets," which I did with my buddy Lou Reed singing backup.

People called me the scandalizer.
The world was my appetizer.
I turned gangs into fertilizer.
King of the New York Streets.
I broke hearts like window panes.
For breakfast I'd eat nails and chains.
To my kingdom I'd proclaim:

King of the New York Streets.
I floored my accelerator
all the way to the equator.
Just a local gladiator:
King of the New York Streets …
People come from miles around
to see my royal tenement crown.
Always up and never down:
King of the New York Streets.
Schools gave me nothing needed.
To my throne I proceeded.
Every warning went unheeded:
King of the New York Streets.
I stood tall from all this feeling.
I bumped my head on heaven's ceiling.
Shooting dice and double-dealing:
King of the New York Streets.
You know, each time I jumped behind the wheel
of a pin-striped custom Oldsmobile,
the guys would bow, and the girls would squeal:
King of the New York Streets....
Well I was wise in my own eyes.
I awoke one day and I realized:
This attitude comes from cocaine lies.
King of the New York Streets.
Well, I was only sixteen years old,
so what could I have known?
In my mind these passing years
the legend sure has grown.[2]

The legend sure *has* grown. And here's the surprise ending, a lesson I learned later than I should have but one that brought me a lot of peace: It's a lot easier being King of the New York Streets when you know that you still report to the King of Kings (see 1 Timothy 6:15). It takes the pressure off. I mean, you still have your work to do, but it's the work your Father wills you to do. It's being "about my Father's business" (see Luke 2:49).

In fact, I just got back from visiting the King of Kings. Every Tuesday in the parish nearby, there's Eucharistic Adoration. So I wander over. I told him about you, and I asked that this book be a blessing for you.

Yo! Rock on!

NOTES

Chapter 2: Rebels and Causes

1. Boudleaux Bryant, "Hey Joe" (Nashville: Sony/ATV Music Publishing, 1953). All rights administered by Sony/ATV Music Publishing LLC, 8 Music Square West, Nashville, TN 37203. All rights reserved. Used by permission.

Chapter 4: A Chosen Few

1. Ricardo Weeks and Maxwell Anderson, "I Wonder Why" (New York: Spirit Two Music, Inc. (ASCAP) o/b/o 3 Seas Music Corporation). Used with permission. All rights reserved.

Chapter 7: Teenager in Trouble

1. Doc Pomus and Mort Shuman, "Teenager in Love." Copyright ©1959 (renewed) by Unichappell Music, Inc. All rights reserved. Used by permission of Alfred Music Publishing Co., Inc.

Chapter 8: Just Dion

1. Alfred DiPaolo, Silvio Faraci, and Sal Pippa, "Lonely Teenager" (New York: Lola, 1960).

2. Dion and Ernie Maresca, "Runaround Sue." Copyright © 1961 (renewed) Mijac Music and Bronx Soul Music, Inc. All rights for Mijac Music administered by Warner-Tamerlane Publishing Corp. All rights reserved. Used by permission of Alfred Music Publishing Co., Inc., Ernie Maresca, and Bronx Soul Music, Inc.

3. Dion and Ernie Maresca, "The Wanderer," 1960. Used with permission of Ernie Maresca and Bronx Soul Music, Inc. All rights reserved.

Chapter 9: From Top to Bottom

1. Greg Shaw, review, "Dion & the Belmonts: Reunion; The Belmonts: Cigars, Acapella, Candy; Dion's Greatest Hits," Rolling Stone, March 29, 1973, www.rocksbackpages.com.

2. Willie Dixon, "Spoonful" (Los Angeles: Hoochie Coochie Music, 1960).

Chapter 10: I Know Jack

1. Dick Holler, "Abraham, Martin, and John," copyright 1968 Regent Music Corp. All rights reserved. Used by permission.

Chapter 12: Reimagining John

1. "Imagine," © 1971 John Lennon. Used by permission. All rights reserved.

2. Bob Dylan, "You Gotta Serve Somebody." Copyright ©1979 by Special Rider Music. All rights reserved.

3. "Serve Yourself," © 1971 John Lennon. Used by permission. All rights reserved.

4. Augustine, *The City of God,* in *Augustine of Hippo: Selected Writings,* The Classics of Western Spirituality, Mary T. Clark, trans. and intro. (New York: Paulist, 1984), p. 456.

5. John Lennon and Paul McCartney, "Revolution" (Nashville: Northern). Copyright ©1968 Sony/ATV Music Publishing LLC. All rights administered by Sony/ATV Music Publishing LLC, 8 Music Square West, Nashville, TN 37203. All rights reserved. Used by permission.

6. See Simon Caldwell, "In interview, Lennon called himself 'one of Christ's biggest fans,'" Catholic News Service, July 14, 2008. Available at www.catholicnews.com.

7. John Lennon and Paul McCartney, "All You Need Is Love," (Nashville: Northern, 1967).

Chapter 13: Bronx in Blue

1. Dion, "I Put Away My Idols" (New York: Wedge Music, Inc., 1983). Used with permission of Wedge Music, Inc., and Skinny Zach Music. All rights reserved.

2. Dion, "I Let My Baby Do That" (New York: Bronx Soul Music, Inc.). Used with permission. All rights reserved.

Chapter 14: Getting to the Essentials

1. See Augustine, Sermon 131.

Chapter 18: Truth Decay

1. Dorothy Parker, "Bohemia," in Complete Poems (New York: Penguin, 2010), p. 120.

Chapter 20: King of the New York Streets

1. Dion, "Born to Cry" (Boca Raton, Fla.: Bronx Soul Music, Inc., 1962). Used with permission. All rights reserved.

2. Dion and Bill Tuohy, "King of the New York Streets." Copyright ©1989. Used with permission of Bill Tuohy, County Line Music, and Skinny Zach Music. All rights reserved.

About the Authors

DION DiMUCCI is a multiplatinum recording artist, Grammy nominee, and inductee in the Rock and Roll Hall of Fame. His hits include "Abraham, Martin, and John," "Runaround Sue," and "The Wanderer."

MIKE AQUILINA is the author of many books, including *Love in the Little Things, Angels of God, Roots of the Faith,* and *Understanding the Mass.*